WOMEN IN NATURE: AN ANTHOLOGY

Created by Carol Clouse

Edited by Carly Attanasio

LOUISE GRACE PUBLISHING

Women in Nature: An Anthology

Copyright © 2014 by Louise Grace Publishing
Published by Louise Grace Publishing
Created by: Carol Clouse
Edited by: Carly Attanasio

Cover Design by: Carol Clouse
Cover Photography by: dennis wojtowicz photography
Back Cover Photography by Kathleen Patrick
Digital Photographic Assistance by: Amanda Condict
Cover Art by: Carol Clouse
Author profile pictures provided by respective authors

Interior Design by: Carol Clouse
Interior image credits are cited with the individual images
Proof Reading by: Sharon Ziegenhagen
Technical support and conversions by: Wingspan Press
Interior Formatting by: Wingspan Press

Louise Grace Publishing
Reading, Pennsylvania 19605
www.louisegracepublishing.com

Printed in the USA.

1st edition printing May 2014

ISBN-13: 978-0-9897367-1-8

The WIN
Women in Nature
Series

In honor of the earth and skies...
And the connectedness of all
living things

Table of Contents

Feature Contributors are in bold

Introduction

We are delighted to introduce you to the WIN – Women in Nature anthology series.

The concept for this project was inspired by the desire to unearth the female voice in regard to women's relationship with the natural world. Certainly, women have a presence in the various venues and issues of 'eco-culture' throughout the world. There are, however, amazing women living earth engaged lives with soft strong voices that are sometimes scantly heard and *Women in Nature* provides a venue for these voices.

This first publication, *Women in Nature: An Anthology*, is intended to provide an overview of the vast and various aspects of women's relationship and experience with the earth. The stories are pieced together to intentionally portray the diversity of nature's influence and inherent role in regard to our relationship with the earth. Subsequent WIN series books will focus on specific areas of interest and immanent exploration, and will attempt to resource writings from women world wide.

This first book is also intended as an introduction to the format and personality of the WIN - Women in Nature series, as an anthology which will combine true stories from a vast demographic of women, as well as chapters from several key featured contributors in each WIN book.

The stories in this first anthology come from across the North American continent, from women like you, intertwined with chapters by featured contributors of women who truly live their passion. Their unique relationship with nature defines their lives, and their stories are particularly compelling and inspiring.

AN ANTHOLOGY

The WIN series is not a feminist venture, but it is rather the celebration of the unique female experience. Women are different creatures from men, and their relationship to nature is internalized and manifested accordingly. Women explore, interact, and problem solve differently. Their response to environmental controversies and their view of the human beings' role on the earth is a perspective worthy of consideration.

These stories will entertain you - as any good story should - but we also hope you will find these writings to be resonating, intelligent, informative, thought provoking, and inspiring. We are grateful to all the women who initially stepped forward to submit stories - to a new small publisher - for our vision of this pilot book, ***Women in Nature: An Anthology***.

Welcome to the WIN series!

Carol Clouse

Wait A Bit

By

Kelly Kittel

One of the 99 reasons we moved to Costa Rica in 2007 was so our children could experience its many splendid creatures before they're gone. Sadly, most of the indigenous critters in Costa Rica are, indeed, endangered and could disappear within my children's lifetime. I know of this firsthand, because in 1987, my husband and I traveled to Costa Rica from Jamaica, where we were both serving in the Peace Corps. Andy worked with yam farmers in a town called Wait-A-Bit and I taught environmental education for the Jamaica Junior Naturalists. By that time we'd been on the island for almost two years and were both dismayed by the dreadful state of Jamaica's wildlife- its coneys, boas, manatees, parrots, crocodiles, and sea turtles all hiding out on the endangered list.

We approached Costa Rica like environmental refugees, having heard so much about its parks and wildlife, and headed straight for mecca— Monteverde. We hiked into the renowned park daily, rarely encountering any other people. We tip-toed under the scolding white-faced capuchin monkeys, marveled at the butterfly and birdlife fluttering around us, and craned our necks until we found resplendent quetzals nesting high up in the verdant canopy. One by one, we checked off the exotic species we'd come to see until there remained only one.

On our final day in the park, we abandoned the trail and beat through the bush, staying until dusk cast its spell on the forest and I began to think about jaguars. At last, Andy spotted our quarry—the Golden Toad, a fluorescent orange beauty found only in that cloud forest, endemic, meaning it lived in no other place on earth. Set against a background of every shade of green in the waning light, this bright orange toad appeared like a splash of sunshine. It was April and these small toads were mating in pockets of rainwater which pooled in cavities formed by massive tree roots. We hiked out of the park that night under swooping bats, satisfied and spellbound, fluorescent orange spots intruding into our night vision like the remnants of a camera flash. That was back in the dark ages of film and by the time we had ours developed, we realized we'd needed such a flash after all as all we had on our slides was a bright orange spot in an otherwise green background.

Many years and four children later, I was lounging in the comfort of my Oregon living room watching TV when I bolted up from my chair with alarm. The Nature Channel was on and I'd just learned that after that year, 1987, the golden toad was never seen again. Scientists assume that the bright toad succumbed to the many pressures of pollution and a changing climate that have claimed the most sensitive of amphibians worldwide. But when I learned of its fate, I felt like I'd lost a friend. I believe that you won't miss what you've never known, so we took our kids to Costa Rica to begin their love affairs with the likes of monkeys, scarlet macaws, and sea turtles-but not with golden toads.

We were lucky to live near a prime nesting beach for olive ridley and black turtles with an occasional leatherback. Many nights after dinner we checked the tide chart and if it was high, we strapped on our headlamps and drove our quads through the jungle to the deserted beach with any combination of our four children who didn't have homework. On our playa, there were usually one or two guards lurking around, keeping watch over the property by the developer who owned it, and at Christmas and Easter, many Ticos (Costa Ricans) camped under the trees. Typically, however, we were alone with the waves and the stars.

We'd kick off our flip-flops and head for the high tide line, strolling along the warm water's edge, our bare feet sending cascades of phosphorescent creatures in a bioluminescent light show before us. Turtles nest at high tide so they don't have to lumber up the beach too far from the ocean in an effort to avoid predators. Whenever we spotted the tell-tale turtle tracks - like a single tire tread heading up the beach - we followed with excitement, hoping to find a female digging her nest at the other end.

If we did, we'd set up camp nearby. I'd pull a cool, white cotton sheet from our backpack and spread it out on the still-warm sand, then offer up some bug spray and snacks. We'd lie on our backs and wait a bit, enjoying a moon bath. We picked out all the constellations we knew and watched falling stars for up to an hour while the turtle worked, using her powerful back flippers to dig a perfect, flipper-deep hole. She'd rock her shell back and forth to scoop up every last bit of sand she could reach, flinging it far and wide. You haven't lived until a sea turtle has flung sand in your hair.

Image provided by Kelly Kittel

Once the digging was done, she'd sigh and rest for a moment. We'd crawl over behind her to watch her deposit some of her clutch of about 100 ping-pong-ball-like eggs. Each egg was squeezed out of her cloaca, falling wetly into the hole until it was filled with glistening white eggs. Then we'd retreat to our sheet while she quickly filled it in, flipping sand all around her as far as she could manage in an attempt to camouflage her nest. Unfortunately, many Ticos and animals love to eat turtle eggs. While she makes a valiant effort to hide her babies, it is impossible for her to cover the wide tracks made by her shell and flippers as she heaves her heavy body back down the sand to her saltwater home. This path serves as a distinct road map to anyone or anything looking to find her babies. Once back in the sea, the turtle sheds gravity like a bad dream and swims away with great speed and agility, never pausing to look back.

In the eight months we lived in Costa Rica, my kids watched so many sea turtles lay their eggs, they could all give guided tours, including Bella, who was four. I hope some day they'll be able to bring their own kids to our beach, spread a cotton sheet under the night sky, and remember the familiar whoosh of warm waves kissing the sand while a mother sea turtle sighs nearby, her salty tears flowing from the effort of ensuring the survival of her species.

About Kelly:

Kelly Kittel currently lives in Rhode Island with her husband and the two youngest of their five children where she walks or swims the beach daily but sees no sea turtles. Some of her other essays about creatures were most recently published in 41N magazine and Gold Man Review and her first book, Breathe, *will be published on May 14, 2014. She is currently writing a travel memoir about living in Costa Rica and writes a blog which can be found on her website:* www.kellykittel.com.

At Her Mercy

By

Amy Attas

If I hadn't gone on the hike by myself, I would have made better plans. But with no dependents and no one to impress, I was free to take chances.

Earlier, with my boyfriend in the car, circling and u-turning, searching for the trailhead, I'd felt ill-prepared. But once he drove home and I was alone, all my disgraces were private; all my concerns not worth mentioning. It wasn't until Day two that I started to go crazy. Day one was a breeze.

I reached the Pesuta (a wrecked log barge I'd marked as a mid-point) way ahead of schedule. She breached from the sand like a whale out of water, and I fell in love. I found my first night's cabin before lunch. If I'd had company, I would have hesitated about building a fire inside the cabin, on the sand floor. I would have worried when the cabin filled with smoke and spilled out every crack. Instead I chuckled. When I melted my boot trying to dry it, I didn't get embarrassed, and when I scalded my skin on a baked potato, I got a Band-Aid and forgot about it. I didn't use the wound to show off how tough I was, nor to shirk camp duties.

Day two started just as effortlessly. My smoky fire lasted into the morning, making oatmeal as easy on the coals as on a stove. I packed in haste and didn't have to wait for any late risers before heading out. The wet sand of low tide shimmered in the pre-sun's red glow. But only twenty minutes later I encountered the Cape Ball River, and struggled to cross. I walked its length down the beach, searching in vain for a spot narrow enough to jump. I walked back again, searching for some less-threatening shallows. From my map I'd expected a stream, but this river had white caps, and it rushed to uncertain depths. I considered turning back, but at the thought of quitting I hoisted my pack high and stepped in.

My toes froze, and then throbbed. I pushed forward until the river ran up and around my waist. I stopped. In the cold rushing current it was hard to think. I didn't know what would happen if I lifted my back foot; I might've been carried away. I didn't know if the rock bottom was level, or if it sunk to new depths. My boyfriend would have wisely stated that crossing the Cape Ball was not worth my life. But he was back at the apartment. My legs pulsed in cold pain and I forced a step forward. It took all my strength to remain standing in the flow. I inched forward again, then again, and finally scaled up the far shore.

My attraction to this particular hike on the island archipelago of Haida Gwaii, just south of the Alaskan panhandle, was the congenial nature of the trail. Aside from forest sections at the beginning and end, it ran along 55 miles of beach with no hills to climb or signposts to follow. I liked that I didn't need a map or any prior training. I didn't need to haul a tent, because there were cabins along the route. I didn't need to haul water because there were plenty of streams. But by 10 a.m. on Day two, I no longer thought of the trail as congenial.

The beach was so boring, so long and homogeneous, that appallingly far points of land taunted me as I inched towards them. Even if I picked a gnarly piece of driftwood as a more attainable goal, I found the footprints required to reach it humiliating. I walked with my eyes closed, then looked back to see how straight I'd traveled; I ran, just to feel something different. I talked to myself. I talked to myself in different accents. I developed a sharp pain in my ankle from the **never-ceasing** slant of the beach towards the sea.

Some people listen to waves crashing to help them fall asleep. I will never be one of these people. As a companion, the ocean was incessant – more annoying than a brother who repeated every word you said. The ocean was a trickster, coaxing me close, where the tidal sand was flat, then swirling around to make a sand bar so I'd have to turn back.

I wanted to explore: escape civilization, connect with nature, and feel like I'd accomplished something. By noon on Day two, I'd done all of that. Now my only goal was to get the hell out.

As the day waned and my night's destination remained far-off, I chanced upon a cabin that wasn't on the map. Its porch was littered with skulls, under a sign warning, RESTRICTED: NO ADMITTANCE WITHOUT AUTHORITY. For all I knew, it could have been the home of a runaway convict. I was on Haida Gwaii after all, sometimes referred to as the world's largest open-air insane asylum. I crept in and found it empty. I yearned for a safe companion. On a plank above my head someone had etched "The Foxhole", and that night I slept like Saddam Hussein in a coffin-sized bunker on hideout from armed enemies. My only relief was that I could not hear the sinister thrashing of the ocean, or the fierce flapping of wind.

In the morning, I dressed in silence, but when I emerged from 'The Foxhole' I encountered a gale. The ocean was frothy and seasick with icecaps and sand scratched at my face as it hurtled up the beach on a peal of high winds. I was lucky to be travelling with the wind at my back, but when I stopped to pop a blister with my jackknife, sand swarmed into my shelter and infected the wound. I was gloomy like the sky, and if I hadn't absolutely had to hike that day, I wouldn't have. But I only had food left for one day, and my boyfriend was expecting me. So I stumbled up the beach.

Not everyone was miserable though. A raven hovered two feet above the sand, totally still, surfing on the gale. Then he tipped his wing back and flipped up fifty feet in a perfect barrel roll, for no obvious reason except to have fun. To me that raven seemed part of nature, so it made sense for him to be happy, whereas I felt separate, at odds with the gale.

I marched for hours, taking shelter in some wind-beaten dwarf pines to eat a three-day-old sandwich. When I finally reached the half-way river (which I should have crossed on Day two), I stepped in without a thought and plodded to the other side wet and cold, but no longer scared. I didn't bother changing my wet socks because there were more rivers to cross. I put on my headphones without the iPod, just to block out the storm.

A tiny sign on a tree caught my eye. Was it possible I was only passing the second cabin now? If I was only at the second cabin at 3 p.m. of Day three, it would be almost impossible for me to make the trailhead by the next morning. That broke me. In all of my misery and boredom, it had never occurred to me that I might not even make it. But the sign said "Cape Fife" – the top of the beach. Somehow I'd skipped right past the second cabin. From here, it was a mere six miles to the trailhead, and those miles were through forest. I was done with the beach. I raised my middle finger to the slanted sand, screamed to the ocean, and turned my back on the storm.

I decided to snack inside the cabin before tackling the last six miles and sleeping in a picnic shelter at the trailhead. But this cabin was more than mere shelter. Designed like an aboriginal longhouse, it smelled of other worlds, with thick cedar walls and space to stretch, it was pure tranquility compared to the beach. After an hour inside, it was difficult to leave – even putting my shoes on was repulsive. I decided to stay, wake early, and do the last four hours' hike in the pre-dawn.

At 4 a.m. I packed my things. A note in the logbook cautioned that trees down on the forest trail made navigation confusing, adding it was "better to be late than lost". But I was eager for this adventure and felt impervious to both options – even in the dark.

An hour passed without me noticing. I loved the soft moss of the forest floor and the twists of the trail. But I rounded a trunk and climbed up a bank and suddenly the trail disappeared. Trampled grasses shone everywhere. I turned my headlamp and I didn't know which steps to follow. "Better late than lost" echoed in my brain, but I refused to panic. I walked a slow circle, then widened my search carefully. I found a marker and started off again. I realized I was going backwards, spun around and sprinted to make up time.

I lost my way again, and although I was frustrated by the delay I didn't worry. If I'd found the trail once I'd do it again. I walked a quick circle, but couldn't find its start. I walked another circle and still nothing seemed familiar. I memorized my surroundings, and then took ten paces forward. When I turned around all my markers had vanished. Only then did I realize I'd been lucky to find the trail the first time – lucky, not skilled.

I sunk to the ground and waited for the sun. It wouldn't be coming for at least an hour. I turned off my headlamp to conserve power and darkness swooped in. Clouds obscured the stars, and forest obscured the clouds. I forced my breath to stay even. I denied my mind the feast of thoughts that I might be lost forever. Lateness, for its part, was now certain. I listened to podcasts until the battery died, then sang songs and tried to ignore the lonely lack of echo, my voice swallowed up by thousand-year-old cedars and spruce. Every ten minutes I'd wave my fingers in front of my nose to test the light. It was unnerving when I couldn't see them. All forces wanted me to doubt that the sun would ever rise again; I struggled to think of anything else.

A breeze rattled through wet branches and through my fleece. I was getting cold, and tired of having wet feet. I was going to miss my ride. I was never going to be found.

The fear built and built, but then a curious thing happened: I started to feel calm.

I stopped feeling angry at nature, like a teen to her mother, and realized that I was an extension of her. In this total darkness, I was obliterated. I was not of the race that invented automobiles or the Internet, I was a mere organism, a collection of molecules, alive one moment, fertilizer the next. I wasn't alone; I was a freckle on the true powerhouse – Earth.

I have always been disappointed by sunrises. But sitting in tense meditation awaiting the first pale hint of light was something quite different. Hallelujah! It is a miracle as glorious as creation itself that the sun rises for us day after day. When the light was strong enough I took a few cautious steps forward and chanced on the trail. I finished those six miles, but I was a damp, neurotic mess, crawling under fallen logs and limping through puddles.

My boyfriend was late to the trailhead, and when he finally rolled up he treated me like the gal who'd left him four days earlier.

"Hey good looking, need a ride?"

I dropped my bag.

"You'll never believe my morning," he continued, "I got locked out of the apartment. I had to kick down the door. It was so early – before seven."

I stared.

"Hold on, are you limping? Let me take your bag. What happened? How was it?"

About Amy:

Amy Attas is a graduate of York University's Creative Writing program. Her stories have appeared in anthologies by Summit Studios and Cumulus Press, and her reviews in The Rover and The Winnipeg Review. She grew up in Pinawa, Manitoba, and now lives on the road, paying the bills planting trees.

A Walk in the Woods

By

Sara Jewell

At the top of the field where the woods push up against the edges of the old, unimproved road, I stand still for a moment in the middle of our morning walk. The field sprawls to my right, undulating towards the spruce plantation while the woods on my left crackle with quiet. There is our red-sided house in the distance and a trail of footprints meandering through the light layer of snow. Here on the east coast, the heavy snow comes in February and March, even April. My husband, who works for the Department of Transportation, claims it always snows on Easter.

In my late thirties, I fell in love unexpectedly, on a blind date, with a man who owns 72 acres of field and woods, open sky and leafy canopy. Born and raised in this river valley, he knows by heart the land I'm still mapping with my feet, eyes, and soul. The morning loop around this large rural property – with the two dogs - begins at the low end of the plantation just beyond our yard. The early December air is frosty and cool while greyish clouds billow behind the tree line and promise flurries this afternoon. The frozen field grass crunches under my boots.

A croaking breaks the silence and I pause to watch a pair of ravens fly overhead. The whup-whup of their black wings beating through the cold air carries down to me and as the sound fades, we carry on.

In her poem, *How I Go to the Woods*, Mary Oliver writes, "Ordinarily, I go to the woods alone,/with not a single friend, for they are all/smilers and talkers and therefore unsuitable." These lines trudge through my

13

mind as I follow my two dogs, noses to the ground, through the rest of the plantation. The dogs love our walks because I pay no attention to them; they are free to follow the trail of rabbit tracks into the copse of poplar trees without my sharp voice spoiling the scent.

Coming to live on this land after 36 years in the city was like piling all my suppressed ideas inside the fire pit in the yard and lighting a match. I became a bonfire of creativity. All I wanted to do was write. Walk, write, write some more, walk again. Every so often, I would come across an essay praising the combination of writing, dogs and walking. It's a logical trinity: If you have a dog, you walk. If you write, you walk. Unspeaking dogs intent on smells and pondering walkers intent on thoughts make natural literary companions. Some humans do not understand the pleasure of being alone but the dogs do. The dogs will disappear into the woods with me.

"When I am alone I can become invisible," Oliver writes in her poem.

Yet on these acres, I am never alone. I am surrounded by pets and wild things: the dogs and cats, a flock of chickens and a trio of rabbits; the colourful crowds at the bird feeders, the ospreys and eagles and a lone cock pheasant; mice and foxes, a black bear and the graceful white-tailed deer who criss-cross the field; and once, a pair of rare mainland moose.

Every spring, a doe gives birth to a fawn in the field behind our home. I read somewhere that the heart drawn by a young child looks like a deer's hoof print. Not a sharp, well-defined print pressed into fresh mud but the shape rounded by a few days of rain or a wet snowfall. Love notes scattered everywhere.

For Valentine's Day a few years ago, my husband gave me a .22 rifle. He thinks his former city girl needs to know how to shoot a gun.

"You can carry this when you walk in the woods in case you meet some coyotes," he said.

At night, we hear them howling across the river where the woods are thicker and there are fewer homes. Only once have I seen a coyote in the woods behind our place, far back, beyond our property line, before it was clear-cut. A long flash of light grey caught my eye and as it turned, I saw it was a coyote, lean and long-legged. It stared at me then loped away, disappearing quickly. When I was living in Vancouver and driving to work at four in the morning, I encountered two coyotes trotting up the middle of Main Street. As my car drove slowly behind them, the closer one stopped and I braked. It turned to look at me and I remember being glad my doors were locked. It was that street-wise look and the unhurried gait of these two inner-city creatures that assured me of their absolute possession of the street. I was on their turf.

Whose turf are these woods? What if coyotes attack my dogs? The questions conjure a picture in my mind: me driving a sharp stick into the neck of the coyote that has one of my dogs by the throat. Would I have the strength to do that? Arms raised above my head, stick pointed downwards, a roar coming out of my mouth. How strong is my protective instinct? How much rage is stored in me for moments such as these?

The Valentine's gift remains locked in its case, unloaded and unfired. I go to the woods for peace. And I go in peace.

I once knew a woman who was psychic, who worked only with animals because humans were too hard on her head, too resistant to truth. She told me about walking in the woods in northern Ontario and meeting up with a bear. She held a conversation with it, thinking her thoughts and receiving his communication as a voice in her head. The bear did not threaten her, she said, and she did not feel afraid. From then on, I've walked in the woods with a pure heart. If I meet a bear, I want it to know I am a friend. I also know that you back away from a bear, don't run, and drop as many items of clothing as you can as a distraction.

"The day I arrive home naked," I said to my husband, "you'll know I met a bear in the woods."

Mary Oliver does not write about walking backwards, naked, through the woods but in her poem she does mention that she does not "want to be witnessed talking to the catbirds or hugging the old black oak tree/I have my way of praying, as you no doubt have yours." I think if I were to meet a bear in the woods, I would put my hands in prayer position in front of my chest and bow slightly, like we do at the end of a yoga class. This gesture serves to communicate that 'my heart acknowledges your heart'.

When my niece, Mimi, was four years old, she learned how to print her name and suddenly, her name was scrawled on every picture she drew. She then went through a phase of drawing hearts. One day, a hand-drawn picture arrived in the mail from her and on it Mimi had signed her name and drawn a heart. A perfect hoof-shaped heart.

Every time I come across deer tracks on the old road behind our house, I search until I find the one that looks like my niece's heart. Taking off my glove, I lay my palm flat on top of it, the heat of my skin melting the snow until my hand rests against the cold, hard ground. The track has disappeared, absorbed into my body, invisible.

"If you have ever gone to the woods with me," writes Mary Oliver in her final stanza, "I must love you very much."

The dogs walk on, flushing a partridge out of the brush with a sudden thrumming of its wings.

"Oh!" I exclaim to the woods, startled, my breath a puff of white in the cold air.

Like love encountered unexpectedly, it stirs a sudden thrumming of the heart.

About Sara:

Sara Jewell is an award-winning narrative journalist whose articles and essays have appeared in various newspapers and magazines across Canada. She has lived in Nova Scotia for seven years and works at a community newspaper, writing columns about country life and the people who make it so interesting.

Featuring: Cindy Ross

Introduction by Carol Clouse

It was many years ago that I first crossed paths with Cindy Ross. I would like to say it was on a path deep in the woods, but instead it was a path of association through a mutual friend. A lasting impression was planted on me, when our friend spoke of how Cindy had hiked the Appalachian Trail with her young children - packing them at times on llamas. I was impressed and inspired.

At 30, I had hiked and car camped whenever I could, but no one had yet introduced me to the world of backpacking. Once initiated, I was hooked. How fortunate Ross's children were to have been introduced to such an intimate engagement with nature at such a young age.

Cindy's latest endeavor involves a new book with the working title, Stories From an Uncommon Education – Lessons Learned Using the Whole World as a Classroom, on how she educated her children *along the trail and through nature.* She is passionate about spreading the word about the natural world and its role in educating our children.

Cindy Ross crossed the 2100-mile Appalachian Trail as a single woman penning and illustrating her first book, *A Woman's Journey on the Appalachian Trail*, in 1982. Her more recent book *Scraping Heaven- A Family's Journey Along the Continental Divide* is the rousing adventure of a family's incredible five-summer, 3100-mile trek over the rooftop of North America, where they used llamas as kid carriers and packers to carry supplies and diapers across the Rocky Mountains.

We now invite you to take a walk with Cindy, and share some of the many paths that she has tread.

Image provided by Cindy Ross

www.cindyrosstraveler.com

Lives Immersed

By

Cindy Ross

All along the Conchetopa Creek in the Colorado Rockies are miles of beaver dams in all stages of construction and deterioration. Behind dry, deserted dams, the silt is built up to dam level, making it clear that it was time for the beavers to move on. Further along the stream we come across an active dam and the difference is visually obvious. If we crouch down to eye-level with the dam breast, even my one-year-old son, Bryce, can see how it raises the water level a few feet. Entrance holes are clearly visible in the beavers' homes. On land, the children run their fingertips over the tooth marks on pointed stubs of trees that the beavers have gnawed down and hauled away- some so recently that the scattered wood chips are still visible.

Because they built a dam where the Colorado Trail crosses a small creek, the beavers turn our previous hop-across ford into a thigh high swim. It's obvious that the beavers are in charge, and they have the ability to radically change a manmade trail in a matter of days.

Tonight, my eagle-eyed daughter is the first to spot the beaver, silently gliding in the pond by our camp. She runs back wildly to our tent, so excited she can hardly speak. Our family is camping by Peru Creek in the Rocky Mountains of Colorado. I have spent enough time in the backcountry to know that when a beaver chooses to emerge, it is a rare gift. I grab the binoculars and cameras and we navigate back to the pond.

Creeping toward the stick dam, we watch as the beaver chews a willow branch with its sharp teeth. Then, sprig clenched in his mouth, it swims to the dam breast and disappears. We wait; scan the pond trying to guess where the beaver will resurface. The kids gasp when the slick round head parts the water and the dark, beady eyes reappear. Sierra is not happy until she sneaks barefoot through the mud to stand closer to the dam. She watches the beaver swim back and forth for an hour. Not until darkness falls and her beaver friend retires for the night, does Sierra skip back to our campsite, saying, "Mama, today was one of the happiest days of my life."

Image provided by Cindy Ross

While we are watching the beavers, a small summer shower moistens the earth, bringing a brilliant double rainbow that stretches right over the beaver pond. A golden eagle soars over our heads, its mighty head glowing from the setting sun. I look at Todd, and we exchange a look that clearly says, "This is what we leave home to find."

Todd and I first took the kids onto the Colorado Trail because it made *us* happy. It's what *we* loved to do. The kids literally came along for the ride. Before long, however, we realized how happy it made them. It is easy to see that the natural world possesses tremendous gifts for the child who spends time in the outdoors and it stands to reason that when you increase the length of stay and the quality of the experience, results will be even greater. There is, however, so much more happening than meets the eye.

Months later, we were visiting friends in southern New Jersey. We had just spent a few hours in the car and the kids were anxious to run around outdoors. Our friends live on a quiet, rural road, and a large field behind their house leads to an expansive scrub pine forest full of winding deer trails and hiding rabbits. A child could look at it as the gates to adventure, like C.S. Lewis's cupboard doors that lead to the land of Narnia.

My friend was anxious to show my children their new program, "Acorn Pond". Her daughter skillfully clicked on areas around the pond and the animals came out and told us what they were doing. When she clicked on "beaver," the computer simply said, "Beavers build dams on streams". I watched Sierra, as a look of slight confusion crossed her face. It brought her back to our Colorado beaver friend: hearing the slap of his tail, seeing the light glisten on his wet fur, smelling the pond water, feeling the warmth of the lowering sun. The computer image didn't reflect that beavers did much more than "build dams on streams".

This is when it hit me; *how much we are teaching our children just by placing the world of nature in their path.* Experiential learning is more comprehensive than a book, more dynamic than a school building, more engaging than a computer program. This kind of learning will stay with them for the rest of their lives, because they have lived it.

Todd and I realized there is much to share in the natural world the very first time we took Sierra out as an infant. When she had the occasional crying jag that makes a parent wonder if it is colic, we would take her outdoors, no matter what the hour, the temperature, or the weather. It isn't necessary for her to see the wind blowing or the light dancing to divert her attention- a pitch-black night worked the same miracle. There was simply something special about going outdoors that actually made her happy. We used this seemingly magical technique throughout her babyhood any time it was necessary.

When Sierra was only four months old, we took her on her first long backpacking trip- the 60-mile Loyalsock Trail in Pennsylvania. We watched Sierra's young senses open wide to all the beauty around her. We saw her stare, mesmerized, at the sparkling sunlight on a lake. We watched her listen to a singing brook and follow the wind as it raked through the trees and fluttered the leaves. We listened to her caw to ravens and fill with delight when they answered. We watched her discover textures like pinecones, big oak leaves, and sand in her toes. When she woke up in our tent, she immediately rolled over and smiled before her eyes even opened. We knew she was happy out there.

Positive experiences like these in Sierra's first years of her life convinced us that taking our small children on a 500-mile adventure across the Colorado Rockies would be a very beneficial endeavor. Sure enough, we see the same effects of the natural world on our young Bryce.

One evening, shortly after supper, he disappears from our camp. I call and call, but I get no answer. I check the area around our campsite. I find him a short distance away, within earshot, but oblivious to my calls. He is sitting in an open meadow in the lowering sunshine. A gentle breeze plays lovingly with his sun-bleached hair. He is lost in thought, staring at a purple aster in his hand as the wind fingers the petals, bending them down, and lifting them up. He is mesmerized by the incredible beauty of the moment. My throat tightens and my nostrils prickle. My God, my children *must* be happy out here. A sunlit meadow, a simple flower, an evening breeze are entertainment enough for my little boy.

From all our experiences long distance hiking, Todd and I feel we know the natural world well. We feel it is our responsibility to show our children as much of this world that we can and teach them as much about it as we can. On this first long distance hike, I made a conscious decision to turn the outdoors into their classroom. It was a decision that would continue throughout our five- summer traverse of the entire Continental

Divide Trail. What began as "trailside environmental education" at the ages of one and three years old would stretch until they were six and eight years old when we would reach the border of Mexico and the end of this long national scenic trail.

On the Colorado Trail, teaching about the natural world is easy. There are the obvious lessons like the one particular day when their 'classroom' is a large burn that our trail crosses in the Sawatch Range. We take the opportunity to teach three-year old Sierra about forest fires- how they start and what happens to the animals in consequence. We point out ditches that the firefighters had dug to try to stop a fire's spread. We look at the rock-hard serotinous cones of the lodgepole pine, whose seeds are so tightly encased that they need the intense heat of fire to open the cones. In the evening, we build a campfire and explain fire further.

I use teaching on the trail to keep my children entertained. One day, we talk about how trees grow, how they are able to stand upright, and how there as many miles underground holding them up as there are branches that we can see. We tell them to imagine tiny straws sucking up water to the leaves. We encourage them to use their imaginations and see images in their mind, a skill that often atrophies as we grow older. Of course, as a parent, you possess a sufficient amount of knowledge so you can share, but we carry field guides and learn together.

Often times we look for things. Once their eyes start looking and they begin to really see, they are never bored.

In the early mornings or evenings, we sometimes get the children to whisper or stop their chatter altogether as we search for deer in the open forests. We look for squirrel nests in the trees when the leaves have fallen off. Along water's edge, we look for ducks swimming and turtles sunning on rocks in the water. We look for fish moving beneath the surface and birds in thickets and briars. We scan alpine meadows for running marmots. In mountain lion country, we search for trees that had strong horizontal limbs that are capable of supporting a large cat. In the mountain's scree slopes, we search for squeaking picas. I explain the animal's habits, like a squirrel, where they get their nest material, what they use their nest for, why it's there, etc.

As my children learn to look more closely and deeply at details, they wonder more extensively. They begin to think and exercise their imaginations. Children are naturally inquisitive and want to learn. The vast arena of the natural world is one of the best places to conduct such lessons. In nature, children make full use of their senses and their instinct to be creative.

On the trail, I am amazed at the extent of my three-year old son's ability to focus on the world within his imagination. He makes up rhyming poems about "Bonemen" and tells long stories about goblins and ghouls. He often hikes ahead of me, spending as much time turning around and looking at me for a reaction as going forward. If he's telling me a story in camp, he follows me around while I do my chores. The most amazing behavior, however, is when he playacts as he hikes.

He finds a stick with a few branches broken off that looks like a crude gun. For half an hour he pretends he's a robber, shooting and making all kinds of mouth sounds. Or he finds a horseshoe and holds it with his shirtsleeve pulled over his hand pretending he's Captain Hook. For an hour he is a pirate, making a deep voice to recite pirate poetry. He does all this while he is walking a normal two and a half mile per hour pace, but he does not walk on the trailbed. The trail is frequently in a ditch, eroded by horses' hooves and hiking boots. He crosses back and forth from the trailbed's ridge to the ditch, to the other ridge, and back down again. He stumbles over rocks and tufts of grass, putting in far more miles than necessary.

He's also oblivious to what is happening inside his boots. I never see his sock tops, just his lily-white ankles. At breaks, I take off his boots and find fabric bunched up around his toes and jammed under his instep.

"Doesn't it bother you to hike like that?" I ask.

"I never feel it, Mama," is his smiling, honest answer.

All these months and years spent on the trail has nurtured an amazing ability for Bryce to creatively entertain himself using his imagination. He has elevated this skill to an art form and it will serve him well.

Once I was busy writing in my journal on the trail in camp, when Bryce yelled from the bushes.

"I've got bones!"

"That's nice," I reply, not even looking up. He makes trip after trip. Huge cow bones so big he can hardly carry them. He sits down and gets out his felt tip markers and draws monsters on the flat areas (pelvic bones are best). He's planning on putting together a puppet show for us. He disappears for more and yells to me to help him.

"I can't carry them," he hollers. "It's too big!"

When he finally rouses me, I discover they are still stuck together! There is dried meat and hair still on them! Of course, he never notices.

Another time Bryce finds a totally dried-up shrew and begs me to let him keep it. It looks as though it is frozen in mid-jump, and my compassionate son's heart goes out to it. Although Todd does not think it wise, I let him hold it by its hard tail just until we reach camp- if he promises to wash his hands. He names it "Thumpkin" and sings and talks to it, telling it how much he loves it for over an hour. I am amazed at what strange, seemingly insignificant things bring children such visceral joy on the trail, and how imaginative they are when they are not stifled.

Spending such massive time in the natural world unleashes all kinds of creative thought and play in our children and as the miles tick by, the gifts are becoming more obvious. But a person is also pulled outward, especially in open country. The scenery yanks us completely out of ourselves. We walk differently. Our heads are up. The expanse pulls our necks up. The muscles in our eyes feel stretched from so much long-reached looking. This is a completely polarized effect that a life in front of a screen produces. Here in nature the mind is free to wander and wonder. We learn to become bigger, broader.

Some of the things my children learn while traveling on the Continental Divide seem to be acquired through osmosis, without Todd or me actually verbally pointing it out. This fascinates me, because I begin to understand how profoundly children are influenced by what they are experiencing or observing without even being aware of it.

We see the same learning-by-osmosis when it comes to rock hopping across a stream. Todd and I watch as the children select stable rocks and judge the distance correctly. They plant their feet with skill and cross with agility and grace. We do not know how much is seeping into their subconscious just by doing as they follow us all these miles. We do not sit down and actually teach them wilderness skills. They might not be adept at manipulating a computer mouse or finding the Old Navy or Gap stores at the nearest mall, but they have picked up other skills along the Continental Divide.

I wonder if knowing how to negotiate a mountain pass and how to ford a stream are worthwhile skills. Will they need to know these to get through life? It is what the experience and the knowledge are doing to their personhood - teaching them creative problem solving, building confidence - so they can go on to do anything their hearts desire. They are also learning self-reliance, courage, perseverance- invaluable lessons for anyone to learn.

Image provided by Cindy Ross

People have wondered: why don't we take our kids to Disneyland like everyone else? In terms of family 'vacations' we're on the opposite end of the spectrum. Our long distance hike is not a getaway. It's an extension of our life, our values- not a departure from life but an arrival. To us, a Disneyland vacation blows by in an instant. Our trek, however, is lasting- rock solid, like the mountains we walk on.

This is how our children's *whole childhood* begins to look and be designed. We strive to continually place them 'out there,' learning and seeking beauty and understanding. What begins as an actual physical path- The Colorado Trail and then the entire Continental Divide Trail, becomes a metaphorical path of their whole childhood.

Besides all these lessons, one of the most impacting and lasting impressions we glean from all these summers on the trail brings us right back to the sound of the slapping beaver's tail, the eagle flying low and the arrival of a double rainbow. Annie Dillard said, "Beauty and grace are performed whether or not we will or sense them. The least we can do is try to be there." The least we can do is show up for 'the show'. This is how we *always* want to live...by "showing up" as often as we can. After an early childhood of being immersed in the natural world, our children have learned that beauty and peace lay just beyond C.S. Lewis's "cupboard door." It's up to us to go find it.

A Healthy Respect

By

Catherine Weiskopf

On a summer day in a fern-laden, deciduous forest of Yellowstone National Park, our family started down a mulch path. Our two young children darted around us, taking in all the sights closer to ground level. Ben, our nine-year-old, squatted next to a small pond as we meandered down the path, giving him time to explore on his own while still being able to maintain visual contact. Suddenly, a multi-colored cousin of the dog darted out of the woods to our right, crossed the path, and trotted behind us to where we had left Ben.

Our then seven-year-old daughter shouted, "Doggie," and set off down the trail running after the coyote. Clearly we had missed something in our children's education while planning for this trip.

We grabbed her, before the coyote could pick up her scent, and yelled for Ben. The coyote stopped parallel with our son, sniffed the air with his pointy nose, crouched into his shoulders, and watched this creature named Ben playing in the water. We frantically shouted for our son and raced down the path towards him.

Ben finally heard our cries, stood up, and turned to face this wild animal staring him down. Having a straight on view of the extra pointy snoot and larger teeth, our young son had no doubt this wasn't a friendly "doggie." With eyes the size of a Frisbee, he raced toward us, certain he was soon to replace Little Red Riding Hood.

This was our first vacation where our kids experienced wild animals of the predator type up-close, with no woven wire or wood separating the two. They had assumptions about animals being cute and cuddly that we weren't fully aware of until we were face to face with them - and their teeth.

We had snorkeled with fish, roamed among the prairie dogs, and spotted an occasional possum tight roping along our back fence; but their experiences with wild animals were white-washed and safe. They viewed animals in the zoo behind safety fences, watched animals on TV, and were entertained by cartoon animals talking friendly to people. But stepping into their natural territory is different.

Yes, Yellowstone was the first time where we felt we were in their home. Yellowstone brimmed with animals capable of doing them harm if they crossed the line. The bison could flip them in the air like a pancake, an elk could shish-kabob them with an antler, and a bear could maul them if they didn't learn a healthy fear. These animals were not out to harm, but clearly had the mass and teeth to do so if necessary.

Healthy fear, respectful fear, is good and was sadly missing from our children's education. Until this experience, we never realized what we had failed to teach them about nature and the natural world around them.

Two days later, at Mammoth Hot Springs, we witnessed a stark example of how this unhealthy lack of respectful fear looks in the adult version. Mammoth Hot Springs is elk rich country, with elk mating calls echoing off the hills at night I've never heard them at night--evenings & mornings, yes.. During the day they seem like reindeer cavorting around Santa's North Pole as they stroll the streets of the old fort.

That day we saw a father trying to get his three-year-old son to stand in front of a grazing elk for a quick photo. An elk with a full rack of antlers that made him look a lot like Dasher. "That's a wild animal, you know, and people get impaled with antlers every year," my husband said as we made a wide path around where the elk stood.

We hear of shark attacks and bear maulings, and may react by not wanting our children to venture into the woods or the oceans. Some people in Yellowstone never ventured out of the protective surrounding of their metal car. There are two sides of the same unhealthy fear. One being the idea that animals are cute and cuddly, and the other is the feeling that terrifying danger lurks in the natural world. Animals are not out to harm us, but they have the ability. Our children have a healthy fear when they know the true nature of animals.

Animals will guard their property.
Animals will defend themselves if they feel in danger.
Animals can consider us as food.
Animals will protect their young if they feel threatened.
Animals don't like humans getting in their space.
And it is, after all, their space and their home.

Our children don't have a healthy fear of wild animals when they imagine them to be the same as docile pets: when they think of bears as cuddly, and coyotes as cute doggies, or elk as Santa's reindeer.

One way for our kids to realize this is to travel among (the animals), (at a safe distance of course), hear the stories of other adventurers and rangers, and to have (safe) encounters of the coyote kind. When our children get glimpses of how animals live in the wild, it finally and completely makes an animal's wildness real and in turn blesses our children with a healthy fear of the creatures with which we share our planet.

About Catherine:

Catherine Weiskopf is the author of three children's books: Lemon & Ice & Everything Nice *from Scholastic,* Adventure is Mathopolis: Estimating and Measuring *and* Adventure is Mathopolis: Parting is Such Sweet Sorrow. *Most recently she co-edited* Pearls of Promise: A devotional designed to reassure you of God's love. *www.cweiskopf.com*

The Rich and Wealthy

Ofelia Faz-Garza

My father was one of those 'chuntaros' people, who wore cowboy boots and a hat and was laughed at often. He was content being the guy who lived paycheck to paycheck and would come home from work to plant watermelon and squash seeds in our backyard, and tend to the chickens and rooster that were our pets. At one point he brought home a goat that he'd found wandering the streets. He was, in my mind, a tacky Mexican.

When I was in middle school my parents invested their hard earned money on 15 acres of land out in the country. They could have bought a bigger house for us but instead they bought that tract of land. I didn't care that it was my father's dream to have his own 'ranchito', a place to farm, to raise his own herd of goats and to be one with his first true love: nature. In my self-absorbed world, that beautiful plot of land - with a small creek running through it that had an oasis of trees and plants growing through its mid-section and mesquite trees bordering the road - was my newest burden. It was the reason we would have to stay in our little dump of a home and I hated it.

I eventually went off to college because I believed that, unlike my father, I had dreams and ambitions. I would graduate from a university with a degree in business and go off to make my fortune. Then I'd be able to get my parents a nice house and car, help my sisters and brother with their schooling, come back to my neighborhood and start to make things better. Money was the door and my degree was the key.

A couple of years after graduation, when I was neither in business nor making the big bucks I'd dreamed of, I found employment at the local school district working with high need students and their families. My hours were long and stressful and the pay was pretty paltry, but I loved what I did. I was at a turning point in my life where I was slowly beginning to move toward the idea of a life fulfilled rather than a financially filled life.

And, I was fortunate to have found the person with whom I wanted to share my life.

It was the night before our wedding. My soon to be husband and I decided on a modest celebration, so my sister volunteered her backyard. Our ceremony would be small and intimate,and the party afterwards would be filled with our favorite music and homemade Mexican food. As we put up tables and chairs and hung up decorations, my father gave us an early wedding present - a small cactus in a terracotta-colored plastic pot. He hadn't re-potted it in a nice pot; he hadn't put a ribbon around it; and I would bet money that the price tag was probably still stuck to the pot's bottom. Those were the sort of gifts we came to expect from my father.

The day of our wedding, everything looked beautiful. Things were simple and casual but everyone enjoyed a wonderful night. We laughed; we ate; and we were surrounded by love and friendship. And then my husband and I noticed it. That unappreciated little cactus bloomed a most gorgeous yellow flower.

We both began to get teary eyed, because it reminded us of the family and friends who weren't with us anymore. The flower shriveled away by dawn's light as the party waned.

That simple little cactus became one of our prized possessions and moved with us when we bought our modest little house the following year. We moved it into a larger pot and it grew some but didn't flower. It didn't matter because the beauty of that one flower on our wedding night was enough to keep our love for it thriving. Six years later we noticed something growing on one of the 'pencas' or paddles and we excitedly waited for another flower. Instead it formed a heart shaped-paddle. We watched it with intrigue because it started to grow at the same time we were expecting our first child. Once again this spiny cactus was mirroring the splendor in our lives. Mother Nature was manifesting herself in our lives through one of her most simple creations in a most spectacular way.

It's been fourteen years since my father gave us that cactus, and in those years our ninety plus year old home has been blessed with three beautiful, wild-haired daughters, two tiny Chihuahuas, a departed Great Dane, a small flock of ducks, various fish, several birds, and quite a few feral cats. We have a yard filled with roses and lavender, a majestic pecan tree and luscious fig tree, and garden boxes that have graced us with summer bounties of eggplant, okra, cucumbers, greens and cilantro. Compost bins grace the corner of our yard; rain barrels are hidden in little nooks and crannies; and our yard is furnished with pieces my husband has made from reclaimed wood.

Now I am the one wearing peasant blouses and skirts or Mexican dresses with huaraches; my hair in 'chongitos and trenzitas', little ponytails and braids, with big hoop earrings sharing a lobe with my tragus piercing. I'm the 'tacky Mexican', the nerdy, granola tattooed Mexmama whose been called a chuntara for delivering with midwives. I am my father's daughter.

We live in our own little urban paradise and our little ones love nature. They know almost instinctively when our plants need water and will sit and touch the leaves with gentle caresses. I catch them sniffing the basil and sneaking bites of green onion tops when we're not looking. They play hide and seek in the duck coop and know how to crack pecans like an expert. They sit quietly to look at the woodpeckers that tap their Morse code calls early in the morning and scream at the top of their lungs when they catch a glimpse of the neighborhood hawks who have been known to catch an occasional squirrel in our backyard.

And that rancho that I hated so much has become our sanctuary. We go to help my father feed the goats and clean out pens, and make plans for the small parcel of land that my parents have now given to us. I've discovered that nature recharges me. It feeds my body; it nourishes my soul; it connects me to a long line of ancestors who also worked and cared for the land they were charged with.

I owe all these joys to the simple misunderstood man whom I call Father. He taught me to see the beauty in this world of ours,; to see that a life spent surrounded by nature is a beautiful and rich one. He taught me with a sad little plant that the world can be complex and tiresome but that our lives don't have to be when we take time to walk humbly with bare feet upon our glorious Tonantzin, Pachamama, Gaia, Terra, Mother or whatever other name one uses to describe this earth.

About Ofelia:

Ofelia Faz-Garza is a free-lance writer and poet who lives in Texas. She is a member of the DFW Latino Writers and North Tejas Writers groups. Her work has been published in the Voces de Oak Cliff Chapbook. She has a degree in anthropology and works as a community advocate.

The Road Home

By

Grace Peterson

In this part of town one must always be on the lookout, especially at 5:00 p.m. No slacking, no diversions and certainly no texting. As I maneuvered the car out of the parking lot and through the first in a series of green lights, my eyes oscillated from cars to people all moving swiftly to their respective destinations. We are recent migrants from the populated east coast, driving around in the expansive northwest. My passenger made an observation, as it occurred to her that "pedestrians here don't wait for you to stop. They either assume you will or demand that you do by stepping right out into the street." She was right, which was why my stress hormone was going through the roof.

Once I drove over the railroad tracks, I was officially on the Oregon State University campus, where well-lit signage beamed its official mandates like a grumpy professor. On cue, swarms of young pedestrians sailed through the crosswalk on skateboards ahead of the more sluggish students, laden with the requisite backpack and a cell phone in front of their nose.

I saw her just ahead. She waited at the prearranged corner and as I pulled the car up, she opened the door, relieved to gain shelter from the remaining pelts of rain. She showed me a handful of chestnuts she rescued from the sidewalk, but I barely had time to glance at them as I veered the car back into traffic.

Leaving the campus, my exercise segued from dodging pedestrians to joining a train of fast-moving vehicles. Finally, the last vestige of university life, seated in several narrow kayaks, floated on the Willamette River to our right. A chill ran through me as I pondered what it must feel like to be so close to those ominous waters. The mother in me wondered about life jackets and safety, as I tried one last time to steal a glance through the trees at the brave participants.

As I heard about her day, my mind drifted from what I'd left behind to what would be waiting once we arrived home. Silly, I thought. I shouldn't rush things. Relax and enjoy this trip with my daughter.

I took a deep breath. It was easier now that we had turned off the highway and onto the road less traveled. Ahead, the deep gray line ribboned its way up and over the next ridge, bisecting acres of farmland that was tilled and planted a few months earlier, now left to do its growing under the vast Oregon sky.

She spotted him before me since she was unencumbered with driving duties and seemed to have innate radar for such things.

"There he is!"

A jolt of triumph coursed through me as I briefly caught sight of a stately, flawlessly poised heron. Alone in the center of the field, he had become the highlight of our homeward journey.

He lived out there somewhere with his family. Perhaps near the swampy area on the other side of the highway. But often he'd come to this particular field where he'd stand like a guardsman in wait of some unseen intruder. Sometimes he'd be joined by a family member, two of them on patrol, acres apart in the vast nothingness.

Sometimes they'd perch themselves at the farthest reaches, barely a speck on the horizon. Other times, they'd be up close, just a few feet from the road. With no shoulder to pull over, we were forced to drive on, missing an awesome photo opportunity. But we reminded ourselves that herons are wary of humans and would likely fly away before we could get to our cameras.

Good times- trading compressed humanity for vast stretches of sky and earth. It does a heart good, riding in the car with my daughter, sharing the thrill of a wildlife sighting. From the time she and her siblings were small, I made a really big deal about paying attention to what surrounded us outside the car windows. It's paid off.

I drive alone now. My daughter has moved away, embarking on her own independent life. But I think of her daily, as I scan the farmer's field, hoping for that jolt of excitement as I make my way home along that road less traveled, the home of the heron.

About Grace:

Grace Peterson is an author, garden columnist and blogger. She is a member of the National Association of Memoir Writers and the Association for Writing Excellence and is published in several anthologies. She lives in western Oregon, sharing a home with her husband (and four furry felines) while their four grown children come and go. Reaching is her first book. Her gardening memoir is slated for publication later this year. www.gracepete.com

All the Others

Carly Attanasio

The most formative moments of my life took place on the back of a horse. I owe much of the development of my confidence, self-awareness and moral compass – to horses. Keen self-awareness is especially important when piloting a twelve-hundred pound "mind-of-its-own" over a four-foot timber fence. As hooves thunder over grass or sand, I recite key nuances silently and with composure: Is my upper body positioned correctly? Are my hands carrying just enough pressure to his mouth? Do I have enough contact with my lower leg to maintain balance? Oh, and am I still breathing? I had better sift through my equitation-repertoire quick and get this right, because there are approximately four seconds until take-off...hopefully involving both horse and rider.

Horses did more than just cultivate my skills and ability for a sport, however. They taught me how to listen, how to interpret subtle queues, and how to discover and nurture a deep-seated respect for animals and the natural world. Even as a child riding my pony bareback through isolated Pennsylvania woods, I felt an overwhelming sense of responsibility and respect for my surroundings. I knew there was something special about feeling my pony's hooves sink into the soft bed of orange, fragrant pine needles, or sensing his body tense at the sign of wildlife masked just beyond the trail's edge. He taught me to listen closely and heed the communication of the non-human world, as we shared our experience with Mother Earth silently, and together. I was humbled by the animal's perceptiveness, and also knew when to obey his messages. They say if you ever get lost while riding, forget using the sun as your compass, forget your disillusioned sense of direction, and throw the reins to your horse. He will take care of you.

I can attest to the validity of this advice after a crisp morning on the hunt field, when I was still all limbs and oblivious to fear. About halfway through the hunt, I was hopelessly left behind an impossibly high obstacle with no way left, right or under. I was sure my pony and I would forever wander through the misty fields of Chester Country and into fox hunting legendry. I looked sorrowfully at the five foot fence. And though my mount was fiercely brave and athletic, his pony physique didn't quite stack up to the slender, track-star legs of the Thoroughbreds. Similarly alarmed, he bolted off into the opposite direction, feeding into an unfamiliar trail. Pull as I might on the reins, he "grabbed the bit", which in layman's terms means he forgot I existed, and continued his charge through the menacing terrain. He moved with such purpose, that I was eventually convinced he might have known something I didn't. Along with that, my arms were also starting to feel like over-exerted rubber bands, so I resigned.

It must have been miles before we emerged from the dense and hopelessly generic woods. It was with fresh sun on my face that my pony led me straight to a small group of other riders, mostly young and on ponies, with their obvious leader being an older woman atop a gargantuan Warmblood. It was obvious we were the stragglers she was gathering up in preparation for a safe escort home.

The sense of relief I felt at seeing them gave me new energy, along with an equally overwhelming sense of gratitude for my courageous little pony. He instilled in me an invaluable lesson of trust, partnership and bravery that morning. As he traversed through that winding trail, I remembered how he made the ride as smooth as possible for me, moving like a sure-footed deer over exposed roots and rock. He navigated strategically around branches that he could have easily fit under, but were much too low for me. How could an animal be so considerate?

That pony and I would go on to utilize those values of confidence, trust and partnership through years of competitive showing. From county level shows all the way to earning a silver medal at the USEF jumper finals in Kentucky, I achieved countless milestones in my confidence, determination and ability to conquer fear. Along the way, I marveled at how in sync horse and rider could be when respect was valued above anything else. These experiences and cultivation of ultimate respect constantly lend themselves to the person I am today.

As I run my hand over my pony's body, I feel his soft fur turned coarse and the angles of his body now more prominent. We no longer navigate steeplechase fences together; the legs that once transported me across hunt fields at breakneck speeds are now stricken with arthritis. I scratch the base of his ear, just above the scar tissue where he lost his blue eye to cancer.

Just as I learned to uncover my strength as a female and individual from my years of riding and partnership, so I have learned to recognize and attend to his needs as age demands. With the inexorable tempo of time, it's my turn to care for him as he did for me all those years. If it weren't for him, I might not have become so attuned to my inner strength and potential. I might not have believed that I could overcome that which makes my palms clammy with sweat, or seems insurmountable. Most importantly, I wouldn't have recognized my place in the world, how it correlates with others, and how our bonds with humans and nature rely desperately on an unfailing foundation of respect and need to care for each other.

About Carly:

Carly Grace Attanasio grew up on the back of a horse. She combines her love for writing and the equestrian sport to convey the joys and rewards of equine partnership. Carly is a recent graduate of Temple University with a degree in English. She is a former grant writer for a non-profit animal welfare organization and currently enjoys all aspects of writing and editing.

Why I Climb

By

Tate Drucker

I know I'm going to regret it.

  I know I will. I always do when my heart starts to race; my legs start to tremble under the strain; and my throat runs dry. Yet I don't regret it when the alarm sounds at 12:40 AM as the snow whips through the air just outside the tent. I don't regret it as the summit looms impossibly far above where I stand at base camp, forcefully spooning oatmeal into my mouth, looking up at the glaciers with a craned neck. The regret and the doubt come when the climb really begins.

  I started climbing, and I thought, *oh, this is fine! Better than I ever imagined!* Inevitably, that gradual uphill suddenly grew endless and steep - steeper than anything I'd ever felt - and I thought about how I had days or weeks or even months more of this and it was already burning my calves. My heart was already pounding and I couldn't catch my breath, couldn't feel my fingers and it was only twenty-three minutes into the godforsaken climb. I already regretted it. *What was I thinking?* It's a question climbers grow used to hearing time and time again: so then, why do I do it?

  The answer comes in a few different forms. One answer is that I climb for the summit; for the sheer ecstasy, the wonder, and the astonishment of pushing myself to any particular peak. Or maybe I climb for the feeling of seeing camp on the horizon at the end of a long day of scaling rocks and ice and snow and rain. Maybe it's for waking up at midnight to begin the summit push, with the hallucinations in the darkness that eventually give way to a sunrise reflecting off glaciers and the peak just 200 feet away. Or maybe I climb for the sensation of watching the dirt go down the shower drain after two weeks on the mountain, or for the smell of cheesy tuna pasta wafting into the frigid air as its stirred over an open fire. All of that makes climbing worthwhile. There is an unparalleled beauty in the rewards of a hot meal, or running water, or the sunrise from a granite cliff at 5:00 a.m., but there is pain in the injury, in the storms that roll in, in walking for seventeen days just to be told to turn around.

If you are a climber, you understand. Climbing is terrifying — not necessarily due to the threat of altitude sickness or avalanches or the very real possibility of breaking my neck. Climbing is often daunting because it's a mental battle. To be surrounded by the elements, susceptible to a mountain's power that can be more relentless and destructive than even the greatest mountaineers could ever expect. It's about spending days or weeks following the ritual of sleep, walk, eat, drink, walk, sleep, drink, walk, survive, all while circulating back to the voice in my mind saying, *I can't do this.*

Someone once said that if we did everything we're capable of, we'd literally astound ourselves. I've come to realize that maybe the simple answer as to why climbers climb is because we fall in love with — or become addicted to — that sense of astonishment.

It's because of that that I dedicate a massive part of my life to climbing mountains. There is the pain, both physical and mental. There is the regret and pure doubt. There is the intensity in which I believe that I cannot do what I, quite simply, can do.

But then there is the sunrise over the snow. There is the humbling gratefulness of a boiling cup of tea and the sensation of taking off the boots, the layers, and lying in a sleeping bag. And then there is the discovery of myself standing where I've spent months or years dreaming of standing, and I can't explain it, but I know that's where I'm supposed to be.

So, that is why I climb. And I climb, and I climb, and I climb into the clouds, until I am looking down on them.

About Tate:

Tate Drucker is a San Francisco based freelance travel photographer who embodies the phrase, "home is where the backpack is." She began a lifestyle of traveling, shooting, climbing, and embracing the outdoors as early as age 15, and has been avidly exploring the seven continents since.

A Stinging Reminder

By

Sarah Richer

It was 2003, and I was rocking my field work 'uniform': a stained pair of worn-out khakis, an oversized t-shirt I otherwise wouldn't wear in public, a thin button-up long sleeved shirt, mud-caked tall rubber boots, ponytail, and a ball cap. Hot to trot! I was part of a matching set, too - one of a five-person crew on a government contract, combing variously sized woodlots and small forests in southwestern Ontario.

The work was minimum wage, and consisted of long days and early hours. I lived a 45- minute drive from our meeting place, and we had to drive anywhere from an additional half hour to an hour each morning to the different work sites. Since we had to be at the work sites by dawn, I had to get up at what can only be described as dark o'clock. The areas we worked in were dirty, hot, and swampy; they were riddled with biting insects, overly-friendly ticks that carried Lyme disease; often thick with poison ivy, stinging nettle, spiky raspberry cane and thorny-leaved prickly ash.

I fell madly in love with it.

To other families I knew growing up, nature was a scenery backdrop on road trips, or something getting bulldozed in a far away country. But for my family, nature has always been a relaxing, accessible escape. My father would take my siblings and me on hikes in local conservation areas. For me the outdoors was an enormous playground, library, and cage-free zoo. It harbored endless options for exploration at my own pace; a fertile ground for growing questions. One of my favorite activities was peeking under logs for salamanders and capturing crayfish in creeks. Besides allowing me hands-on interaction with wildlife, it let me witness and physically feel how my presence and actions influenced wildlife, and I feel fortunate for that.

There at that summer job, I felt blessed for the opportunity to experience my childhood playground again; this time through more mature awareness and an expanded ability to interpret my surroundings. Parts of my brain typically dormant were roused to life in the woods, and each day came with a new dose of joy and awe from something I may not have otherwise easily observed or been aware existed: The fresh lemony scent of spicebush; a Yellow-billed Cuckoo approaching inquisitively; a chubby fox cub scurrying into a den; the nest of an endangered Acadian Flycatcher; a coal-black and bright yellow forest millipede the length of my middle finger. Anyone who paid attention could never be bored.

We were collecting data as part of a study to monitor the hatchling success and nest parasitism rates between woodlots with different wood harvesting techniques – a welcome switch to something meaningful from past work selling eventual landfill fodder, or slinging alcohol over a bar while pretending to be interested in creepy patron stories. It tickled my brain to see so many cool plants and be so close to wildlife.

A local TV crew was obtaining footage on our nest-searching efforts to accompany their story on Canada's federal government passing the Species at Risk Act. They would ask us to walk away from the camera down a trail, or showcase someone with a telescoping nest- monitoring pole with a mirror mounted on top, or one of us recording observations on a GPS or clipboard. As the heat required me to drink lots of water, inevitably nature called.

The TV crew continued filming my teammates; I excused myself and wandered away until I was confident I was out of hearing range and would not be accidentally caught on camera. I scanned my chosen spot, confirming an appropriate gentle slope, an absence of poison ivy, stinging nettle or anything thorny (I suddenly identified with dogs turning in circles prior to going pee). I slipped down my pants and enjoyed the beginning of relief.

That is, until mid-stream – "OW!" A horrific sharp stabbing pain just south of my lady bits immediately followed with another on my left butt cheek. I looked behind me and saw a river of yellow jacket wasps pouring out of a hole in the ground! My pelvic floor muscles came through and I hauled my pants up pronto, but not fast enough to prevent two more painful stings located about four inches off the mark. I had been stung before so I knew I wasn't allergic. Allergy or no, it turns out pain feels more acute in an area not accustomed to pain. The hurt made me momentarily forget about the filming – I hollered what was probably all manner of unladylike phrases as I ran away from the wasps, praying they were not following me. Thankfully, the crew was on a break and the cameras were off. Either that, or the cameramen were fibbing and there's a video floating somewhere on the Internet of a crazed woman shouting about wasps and hobbling through the woods with her pants half down.

That experience has not at all diminished my enjoyment of the outdoors. But, the less human influence visible in an area, the greater my delight; especially considering the chance that a human presence is capturing footage of the wonders of naturebiting me in the ass.

About Sarah:

Sarah Richer is a naturalist with over a decade of experience conducting breeding bird and species at risk wildlife surveys, and a lifetime of experience indulging her geeky side searching outdoors for all creatures great and small. The stress of struggling in the short-term contract world of field ecology is greatly offset by delighting in the company of her nephews.

Bared Soles

By

Carol Clouse

My bare feet sink into the moistened grass and soggy soil, and my skin absorbed the water that was spilling from the sky. My mother had told me to take my brothers outside to play.

"But" I questioned, "It's raining."

My eight year old mind was swarming to comprehend this motherly matter-of-fact statement. I might just as well have said 'but Mother, it's a beautiful day', because to my mother it was just that – beautiful!

In the pouring down rain of a lightening flashing thunderstorm, my mother would coax my father to load us all into the car for a drive. She couldn't walk. She had been afflicted by polio at the young age of seventeen and her muscles were paralyzed from the waist down. Her toes would no longer squish down into the moist earth, but she encouraged her children to revel in it – in all that is the outdoors.

Our greatest summer thrill was to sleep outside on the back porch, an extension of a day already spent outside. There is surely a tad of irony in my lifelong profession as an architect, where structures are designed and built to enclose people inside barriers of windows and walls. A few years ago I found myself inside four off-white walls - of canvas.

A new chapter in my life had begun by way of an experimental move to remote northwest Montana, and a canvas tent was my home for four months. My 'back yard' stretched beyond the 20 acre parcel into miles of Montana National Forest which yawned east over mountainous terrain to Glacier National Park. Grass and brush flowed among pine trees that I would come to know more intimately as spruce, tamarack, lodge pole, white pine, hemlock, and cedar. The critters that occupied this vast expanse consisted of deer, elk, moose, wolves, black bears, and grizzlies. Did I mention the mountain lions? Yet in my canvas enclosed bedroom, I fell into blissful sleep with my dog at my feet, my boyfriend on one side, and a can of 'Grizzly Bear Pepper Spray' on the other.

In the woods of Montana, living existed there on the earth and it was a purposeful event to go inside an enclosed space to do a task, such as showering, peeing or sleeping. We cooked outside and ate outside, and we sat around the fire, communed, commiserated, and laughed out loud - outside. There was another time where I experienced this sensation of life lived outside. It was the summer that I volunteered for a week long helper stint at a wilderness survival class in the woods of New Jersey.

I pitched my two-man tent - for one - in my selected spot in the woods, and furnished it with my sleeping bag, extra clothing, personal toiletries, and my writing journal. The class kitchen was an open air structure with a roof to keep things dry and to keep the kitchen help shaded from the August sun. I would've thought the woods themselves would serve as our compostable toilet, but with almost 100 people in attendance, there was a row of 'porta-potties' down the dirt road, providing a civilized service for this basic need.

I talked with students outside. I sat in on lectures, ate my meals, worked on fire making skills, helped with kitchen prep duties, and bathed in the cedar tree lined pond – outside. The only time I spent inside my tent was for a change of clothes or for a good night's sleep.

Life was lived – outside.

When I had first arrived at this wilderness class, I had noticed that several instructors and veteran volunteers were walking around barefoot. Their feet were filthy, and I thought it a tad repulsive. I donned my basic black flip-flops, and I felt I fit in. There was a quarter of an inch of rubber between the soles of my feet and the earth - an insulating barrier keeping me clean, protected, yet disconnected.

I was free of walls and windows, but I was still insulating myself from the earth. It had been many years since my infant feet had run freely in the grass, and my childhood toes had felt warm summer mud ooze between them. My feet were almost always insulated. Footwear or man-created walking surfaces have separated me from the touch of the living earth.

Our developed world is covered with insulating layers and the heel-toe kiss of the shod modern foot walks briskly and abruptly on these hard unforgiving surfaces. Concrete walkways are poured all over paradise, as static paths lead us into the boundaries of our homes - into enclosures of walls and windows. We walk from asphalt to concrete in a linear unconscious stride, arriving at the entry door and mundanely walking inside. It is often a path of traverse that offers no compelling call to pause and take account.

The world we are born into is the world we come to accept as the protocol of human existence. The line between the 'natural' earth, and the fabricated context of the human created environment, becomes a stark line of birth circumstance. Walls envelope us in all four directions, and we are cut off from our human relationship to the earth. Windows provide glimpses of the outside, where the rest of the world is alive in its endless connections and cycles. But our feet walk on flat manufactured floors, and occasionally we walk outside.

Back at the survival class, during the sweltering days of August, I continued to don my basic black flip-flops. Then the volunteers were called upon to participate in a demonstration of awareness for the course lecture on camouflage. We gathered together in an area away from the students and began to prepare for our masquerade. Pieces of charcoaled wood were retrieved from last evening's fire pit, and clay and mud were resourced from the ground around us. We wore minimal clothing of underwear or bathing suits, and began the process of painting ourselves with the earthen materials. A few leaves, twigs, and grasses were attached depending on which background we desired to blend into. Shoes were removed.

Each volunteer situated themselves in the bushes, trees, and grounds around a small open grassy area. We were not hiding behind objects, but were vulnerably visible in our blended bodies of camouflage. I lay in the leaves, with my head propped up against a tree. I wanted to see the students walk past me, and witness their unconscious passage. I was immersed into the earth like one melts into a lover, the way in which you cannot decipher where one entity ends and the other begins. I was connected and content. I felt a sensation of innate belonging, and any sentiment of repulsion dissolved and dissipated. She was fertile, not filthy, and I was a part of Her. I was Her.

The course instructors walked down the dirt pathway and lead the students into the open area. The students walked past the nature-fused volunteers, oblivious to our presence. They were conditioned from their paved landscapes, not to pause and consider. They walked by and moved on, and gathered in the clearing. The lecture began about awareness, routine, and being present. After a while the instructor indicated to the students that the volunteers were right there, all around them. The jumping up - and jumping down from trees - began, as students also jumped.

I was barefoot and mud covered.

I went to the pond and scrubbed off the earthen layer. Then I walked back to my tent in my flip-flops. I sat on the ground by my tent, and observed that my foot wear had now taken on a foreign and filthy identity. I took them off, propped them against my tent, and walked barefoot down the dirt trail.

Walking on earth's forgiving floor - spongy with layers of moss, mycylenium, and composting leaves of fall foliage – the morphing fertile soil moves and responds as the bared sole rolls its toe-heel dance on the earth.

And that is how we get beyond our own circumstance. We walk out the door and touch down on planet earth, and send our children outside to play, barefoot in the rain.

About Carol:

Carol Clouse is an architect, artist, and author. Her personal memoir Clouse's Houses, *was recently published by Louise Grace Publishing. She resides dually in Pennsylvania and Montana, and she recently completed her Masters Degree in Architecture at Penn State University. For more information visit www.carolclouse.com*

Featuring: Bernice Ende

Introduction by Carol Clouse

She was wearing her straw hat and was chatting with the folks who wandered by her stand at the local farmers market. I spoke on the phone with Bernice Ende a couple of weeks earlier, and we agreed to meet at the farmers market. I knew it would be easy to find her. It's the Eureka Montana Farmers Market, where in a town of 1100, about six or seven stands can be found set up for business every Thursday, all summer long.

Lady Long Rider, Bernice Ende, was promoting her new DVD and her Lady Long Rider natural skin care products as a way to raise funds for her next horseback riding excursion. She appeared sun kissed and warm hearted. I waited for a break in the meandering traffic, and then stepped in to claim a spot in the friendly flow. Talking with Bernice is like visiting a long lost aunt. She showed me pictures and spoke enthusiastically about her next planned outing. But then a group of young girls walked by, and she politely dismissed herself and walked out to greet the girls. She handed them her picture postcards and introduced herself with ease and confidence. I commented later on how I envied her ability to connect with people and sell herself. She protested my presumption, stating that she found that a most difficult thing to do, and that she had to really work at this aspect of her long rider lifestyle.

It doesn't look like work. It appears as an easy and inherent part of her nature. The question eventually was then posed: What prompted you do this? And why do you continue to go on long solo horseback rides over many months and miles?

The answer Bernice gives is simple but far reaching. She said that she felt that everything in her life had been in preparation for long riding. She felt that it was simply a window of opportunity that had opened.

"I really cannot say it was any one thing," she concluded. "Is it ever? But what continues to pull me, lure me, drive me toward a horizon I will never touch, well that is another matter."

Bernice says it is a calling, not religious, not even necessarily spiritual. It's just plainly something that fits, and something that she had to do. Welcome to the world of Bernice Ende, and her faithful four legged long riding companions.

... *Lady Long Rider*

Image provided by Bernice Ende
www.endeofthetrail.com

Whether or Not

By

Bernice Ende

There it is again.

I was not imagining things. I stopped packing and looked toward the Northwest sky, listening. Yes, it was the rumble of thunderclouds coming in over the line of jagged, red cliffs bracing the north side of the Flathead River as it was running low from two dry summer months. Rain would have been welcomed. Like a morning ritual, I knelt down on one knee beside the two large saddle packs, lacing up the final black nylon strap before loading them onto Essie Pearl's back. Already the wind was taking action. Overhead the sky was wild with disheveled clouds whipping about like youngsters stirring up trouble; like the tails and manes of wild ponies running free all stretched out long and buoyant, decorating the sky with constant change.

Another rumble, closer more serious, was defining the day to come. *Should I stay?* I said to myself as I turned to my three horses that stood quietly, saddled and packed, bellies full of orchard grass. The sun flashed intermittent hot blasts of September heat, reminding me of yesterday's sweltering long day of 90-degrees. It was an assault of flies and mosquitoes, on sweaty horse-backs, and consequentially laborious travel. I would have welcomed a ride in the rain, but a storm with thunder and lighting, *no thank you.*

I stood beside Hart, the tall paint horse, and told him that we would ride today, as I held the bridle rein and studied the sky and wind. I kept thinking, *chances are it will go around us, the winds are from the south west and we are heading due east.*

"We'll be OK", I said to the horses.

As if they understood. As if they cared.

My boot reached for the stirrup, my hand for the saddle horn, and I swung with ease into the saddle.

"Let's go. Let's see what the day holds for us... Essie, Hart, Spirit". I called out in a loud, slow roll call, "Let's go."

Unity took hold with a steady rhythmical stride that fell into a familiar pace. Steel horseshoes struck against the hard gravel road as we headed out into uncertainty, into a wild blistery day of sunshine, clouds and rain; a day of "Weather", as we tucked our tails to the wind heading east, riding out into a gamble.

Image provided by Bernice Ende

This was Tribal land belonging to the Confederated Salish and Kootenai Nation. I was secured with a permit to cross their Tribal lands from Hot Springs to St. Ignatius to Seeley Lake, Montana. The flat open Mission Valley was the expanse before us. To the west was the Cabinet and Salish Mountain range. To the east of the Mission Mountains: the Bob Marshall wilderness the Swan Valley, the "Flathead Alps." Minutes ahead the Sloan Bridge is strapped across the Flathead River, waiting for us to cross. But as we curved around to meet the bridge the horses froze in their tracks, ears fixed, statue still.. Six wide black round eyes (and two blue) were held by the unexpectedness of this outlandish colorful piece of art laid before them.

Sloan Bridge was riddled with graffi. We were unprepared for the visual that the bridge had become. Like a freight car, every square inch of the unpretentious cement bridge was glorified with color, shapes and words. A loud statement that the horses literally tip toed precariously across. The river flowed carefree below us, tall Ponderosa pines swayed with the gust of winds, as we were momentarily held in suspense by this structure of unique beauty. Once across the bridge I could smell the rain before it arrived. A quick cooling of the air preceded the gently descending rain that fell upon us and I dismounted pulling rain gear from the packs wondering if I had made the wrong decision.

Mother Nature. She never has it any other way but her way. No matter what direction you travel in, be it dirt path or paved road, she will have her way with you; dealing the cards, dictating the day, the hours, the minutes with the elements from which myth and mystery are born. No one tells her what to do.

One thing that I can always count on is there will always be weather. Never before have I been so intimately connected to weather. It is an intimacy with life itself that one will never know inside the shelter of four walls or inside a protective shell on four wheels. Accepting this exposure, in your face, submerged in Nature, is the very core of what long riding is. Never before has weather so possessed me. Never before have the actions, mystery, and the challenges of weather demanded my attention as they do long riding. It pulls me to the now and it demands again and again for me to, "pay attention."

As the daughter of dairy farmers, I saw nature's fierce grip in all facets of life. My father's constant checking of weather......the hope and prayers, the uncertainty with which these uncontrollable forces dictated our family farm. I was fascinated by the tornadoes that ravaged the central Minnesota country side each spring and summer. I was terrified by the raging winds that left mass destruction, sweeping up cows and trees and neighbor's barns. I was always afraid for the horses we had on the farm, yet I did not want to hide from it. I wanted to see it. I wanted to feel it.

A maze of straight-line mostly gravel farm roads crisscross the flat open space of Mission Valley. I could clearly see the storm as we moved eastward. A soup kettle of thick gray-black clouds, *possibly hail* I think as they backed up against the fortress of mountains that stood determined to halt the procession, infuriating the pack of renegade clouds. A log jam of clouds rolled over and over onto themselves nowhere for them to go, yet still restless enough to continue. I could see mass after mass of clouds split, then divide, then spill north and south and I knew I had only minutes to find shelter. I pulled the stampede string on my hat to hold it tight, pulled the horses in close and said in a loud determined voice, "Okay, Let's go".

They knew. They always seemed to know, and how can the horses not know. They are *always* in weather. I felt like the ceiling lowered and I must duck or my tall broad-rimmed hat would skim the clouds. We were riding fast, heading for a stand of tall fir trees chased by a pack of reckless renegade clouds. *Fences...damn the fences. Nowhere to get in.* "No Trespassing" signs, locked gates and old rusted barbed wire fences kept me on the road like running down a hallway and all the doors are locked. *I need to get out of this*, I scream in my head. *Just get in somehow!*

I see a loose low spot on the wire, "make it work... Make it work Bernice". In full rain-gear everything is cumbersome. The rain has started and the storm is descending upon us as I hold the two strands of rusty barbed wire down with one foot and coax one horse after another to step carefully over the nasty stuff. Hart and Essie, seasoned long riding horses, are safely in and standing under trees. Spirit, still new to all of this, balks, catches her hoof, and panics.

"Easy, easy, easy" my voice hiding my pounding heart, "It's Okay, come on you can do this".

Still holding the wire with one foot, I slowly folded myself down to reach for her hoof unlocking the mess she is in.

"OK, one more time," I said as the wind mocks my words.

But Spirit was now over the wire and we had the shelter of a grove of dense and stout fir trees. The branches spread out like umbrellas forming a dry canopy below, layer upon layer reaching up the trunk of the trees creating a temporary protective sanctuary. The hard rains scarcely touched us. I moved from horse to horse to loosen cinch straps and removed the heavy packs while we waited. "Thank you", I say mostly to my mother whose spirit rides with me as my protective guardian. But also to the horses for they too were brave and courageous through all of this. They are content to stand under the trees while the storm belts another blow and lightening cracks off to the north. To be warm, safe and dry-thank you.

I feel smug. I feel like any other person that has escaped, made it through the storm, and defied the danger. I ran the risk and I won. I reached into my saddlebags and pulled out a thermos of hot tea and my beat up tin cup. Earl Grey with lemon and honey.

What is it about weather - one of nature's many hands - that I so want so much to be a part of? I want it touching me, holding me in its track of infinite personalities. I want the wind to crawl up my sleeves and the sun to hide under my broad-rimmed hat. I am attracted to the wild invigorating and unpredictable challenge of weathering a storm, of finding myself face to face with natures playful or unforgiving forces, a force that asks, "Do you really want to do this? How determined are you to do this? Well let's see if you can do it."

We were all out of sight, the horses and I, as a car slowly drove by. I could hear the fast beat of windshield wipers as the rain continued in earnest. I am not always so fortunate to find shelter like this. Too many times I have landed in a ditch, exposed for all to see my folly at having been caught in a storm. A pitiful sight as drivers motor past in luxury; eating ,drinking and music playing, with radios warning of a storm, and chatting with passengers or talking on cell phones. And there I was: a pitiful sight indeed, but unwilling to trade places.

Nature has me wrapped in her arms with no immediate escape. She fills me with vitality and nourishment, and offers me mounting challenges. It is the secret to being alive. It's just too easy the other way. I find this life as a long rider interesting, intimate and engaging. It's a no nonsense, cut to the chase life. Direct, persistent, yet reliable. I always know the sun will rise and the sun will set.

I chuckle at the notion that long riding is about "freedom". I come and go as she, Nature dictates, not as I please. I wait for storms to subside, I wait for the wind to let up, and I wait for the snow to melt. I wait to ride the desert in the winter, and ride the mountains in the summer. I can't ride in the sweltering heat or violent storms of wind and cold. I set my tent up according to which way the wind is blowing or the sun is shining. This storm would have held much less meaning to a person sensibly wrapped and secured in a building or motor vehicle. I face fear, doubt, criticism and the very weaknesses that keep most people from ever daring the adventure that often times pull and tantalize them. I simply must be in it.....engaged in all that is this life.

I don't want escape from "civilization" with the notion that "Nature" holds all of the answers. When I look down at the pen and paper I journal on, when I reach for the high tech nylon tent and camping gear I use or the lightweight pack saddle I use, I realize that all of these things have evolved from civilizations where people with ideas and notions and visions have come together to form more ideas and notions and things like head lights and small propane burners. I do not delude myself with "leaving it all behind". Unless one has the knowledge and experience of primitive living skills, it would be impossible to leave behind everything that is not of its original casting and live "naturally". My rides are infinitely easier because of these modern conveniences that I carry. I am not trying to "go back to nature," I just want to be *with* her and learn all that she has to teach me as I make this pilgrimage on earth.

A spider crawled up my rain gear, looking for warmth I suppose.

"Sorry, you can't rest here I must go." I said to it, as I let it crawl down my leg to the earth.

It would have been a good place to camp, but no water for the horses had me up and moving as the sky released the troublesome clouds - dressed in a gentle pink and lavender gown - to complete the day. The curtains were opening on Her evening performance.

The horses began to jig, anxious to get started as I readjust packs, tighten cinches and hand out a three-way-split apple to each of their eager lips before walking them out single file to the fence line. This time we calmly walked over the barbed wire, and I repaired the fence before mounting and turning in my saddle to say "thank you" as I always did for the gift of safety.

I narrowed my attention, focusing on a suitable campsite. I remembered seeing a couple of possible areas along the Crow Dam a mile or so back where we passed on the race in. At that time in the day it was better to retrace steps then to go on into unfamiliar ground. A side trail dropped off into a deep canyon to a steel gate blocking the road and again those damn fences. A man stood next to a beat up older car parked near the gate smoking a cigarette. I rode cautiously up to him to ask if he knew of somewhere I could camp for the night. "Hey just go in through here," pointing to an opening in the fence line," "no one will bother you; they can't get in."

I accepted my good fortune with a smile, nod my big hat and thanked him. The road twisted and circled down into the narrow canyon...

everything so damp and musky smelling. The sky lost its remaining light in less than an hour, and I had little time to think about the dropping temperatures as we once again descended into unknown territory. Before a complete celestial blanket of darkness covered us, I made a quick check of the area we would camp in, not only to familiarize myself with it but also to show the horses.

Where would I haul the water from the creek? Where would I tie the horses? Where was the best grass close to the camp site? Where was the tent to be set up? All questions that run through my mind when selecting a home for the night. Fog slowly settled in, enhancing the cold wet moonless night with the smell of rotting fall leaves as Crow Creek joyfully filled with a stream of fresh water, orchestrated evening music. A fire would have been nice but the effort to build one in this soggy weather over ruled the comfort and ease of my warm dry tent. My three horses were hungry and eager to eat as I hobbled them, ran the pick lines out and covered their warm backs with flannel sheets. My eyes had adjusted to the absence of light by the time I was set up and able to crawl inside my cave to savor my supper.

"Rice and beans and dandelion greens" I sang softly, already nibbling on nuts and cheese and anything else I could get my hands on.

"How are my horses?" I shouted out listening for the jingling and jangling of handmade Romanian gypsy bells that are snapped to each horse halter. If they were troubled in any way, tangled in the rope or not happy in some way, they would whinny back and the bells would ring wildly.

Inside my tent three candles heated and lit the small space easily. I wore a head lamp when I move outside to water and check on horses. Other than that I was embraced by the night's tranquility and sobering darkness. The stainless steel pot of supper boiled on the single propane burner. I stripped down and changed into clean night wear.

As a child I was terrified of the dark. I would never, ever step into a dark room without first sliding my hand along the wall to the light switch or pushing my little sister in before me. I had horrifying, suffocating nightmares that sent me running barefoot, screaming silently down the dim-lit stairs to my parents' bedroom in tears. What happened to that fear I do not know. It fell from my saddle somewhere along the trail. How can I be out here like this without the fear that once bound and gagged me as a child? Did I simply outgrow it? Where and how did I come to embrace the solitary nights so alone and unprotected? It's a mystery answered by these many miles.

It was well past 1:00am when I opened the flap on the tent into a breathlessly still sheet of blackness to make one last check on the horses. Essie Pearl and Montana Spirit were lying down. Hart was standing over by the creek. I laid across Spirit's back and looked up at the dazzling array of dancing stars. Days and nights merged, no longer broken up by mundane routine. I might get my sleep from the day and my food by night. It is a life of accepting . Spirit got up. I passed out attention to the other horses before I called it a day and crawled back into my tent, my home, where I was wrapped in the embrace of Nature.

These years of long riding have provided a platform to discover the core strength, potential, confidence, and resilience within myself. I have found contentment and happiness, all unexpected discoveries in the absence of so much "mankind". It was never my intention to ride out and find this woman that I now have become, it just happened. It was a window of opportunity that I simply and bravely climbed through. I remember the first ride in 2005 and asking myself again and again, "How will I ever go back to normal life?" I felt like I had for the first time, climbed into my own skin. By taking these precarious steps closer to nature I discovered that all of this - the weather, the land, the water, the animals - is also inside of me. I found that I too am filled with Nature.

Image provided by Bernice Ende

Miss-Adventure

By

Annabel Sheila

When I was in my mid-thirties I was in pretty good shape. I walked six kilometers every day, maintained a healthy diet and generally took care of myself. So when my brother challenged me to a twenty-two kilometer canoe trip down one of the most famous rivers in western Newfoundland, I eagerly accepted. There would be four canoes with eight people and the trip would take a full day.

We were going to negotiate the mighty Harry's River. The river was renowned for its salmon fishing, but during the month of August the water level tended to be quite low so we weren't likely to encounter anglers. I figured it would be an awesome way to enjoy a warm summer day in the arms of nature. My roots are Mi'kmaq and I knew my ancestors would have done this trip in a rustic birch bark canoe, so traversing the river in an aluminum canoe should be a breeze.

I have to admit I was a little anxious at first, since I'd only ever been in a canoe a couple of times. But my busy life had taken me away from the oneness with nature that I'd known as a child growing up surrounded by the forest. I couldn't wait to hear the deafening silence one finds in places where humans rarely tread. There would be nothing but wilderness for miles and I knew my soul would be able to reconnect with my body.

My brother had navigated the river many times and I trusted him implicitly. He knew every boulder and bend in that river. Before we set out, I stood on the bank looking out over the majestic river and couldn't foresee any problems other than maybe getting my feet wet from time to time. Ah! Naiveté is bliss.

We loaded the gear into the canoes and layered our clothing to accommodate weather conditions and accidental spills. My brother suggested the best place for me would be in the front of the canoe facing forward so that he could tell me when and how hard to row. It made perfect sense.

At last we were ready. The swiftness of the current surprised me with a gurgling sound as the warm water gripped my ankles. We pushed the canoe out into the river until the water was thigh deep and climbed in. I inhaled the fresh scent of evergreens and wildflowers along the riverbank and it was like a homecoming for my spirit.

We headed downstream, the canoes carried swiftly along on the powerful current. A kilometer downriver we came upon what my brother called a "chute". Of course I had no idea what a chute was until I heard the hiss of the rapids and saw the river ahead of us suddenly drop about seven feet.

"Just sit tight sis, and hold on, you're gonna love it", my brother yelled above the rumble of the rapids. But as the nose of the canoe edged out over the top of the waterfall I was sure we were going to capsize so I did what my survival instinct told me to. I jumped out.

Of course my quick exit caused the canoe to become unbalanced and the next thing I knew I was in the water with my life jacket on and pinned against a huge boulder with the canoe coming straight at me.

My brother shouted, "Get away from the front of the canoe, now!"

I managed to push myself away from the boulder just as the nose of the canoe smacked into it. Apparently an aluminum canoe filled with water weighs about five hundred pounds and would have crushed me had I not moved out of the way in time. For the first time in my life, I realized a person really can drown while wearing a life jacket because the power of the current pushing me against that rock made it very difficult to escape.

Bruised and shaken, I sat on the shore watching my brother empty the water out of the canoe and right it once again. More than a little perturbed at him for not telling me about chutes in the first place, I chided him. "Just how many chutes are we going to have to run today and what was I supposed to do?"

He caught the panicky edge in my voice and calmly explained that if I hadn't jumped out the canoe would simply have shot out over the edge and landed smoothly in the water below. It would have been an exhilarating ride. It was my inexperience with how a canoe behaves in a river that led to our mishap and I fully accepted responsibility. I was determined to push forward. I'd never make it through the next twenty-one kilometers if I didn't.

The sun was beginning to warm my aching body and dry my wet clothing as I resumed my position in the bow of the canoe. I took in the beauty that surrounded me and felt the tension slip away. The current carried us along until the water became too shallow for the canoe. "We'll have to get out and walk a little until the water gets deep enough again," my brother said.

The water was shallow but fast and the rocks beneath the surface were very slippery; it was inevitable I was going to take another dunk. No sooner had the thought entered my mind when out went my feet and I landed on my backside in the river.

My brother snickered at my misfortune and his feet went out from under him. He hit the water with a mighty splash and I laughed uncontrollably at the shocked look on his face.

He sat there laughing and wiping the water from his eyes. "It's nearly noon so we might as well stop for lunch and dry off before moving on."

We pulled the canoe ashore and stretched out on the soft green grass waiting for the rest of the group to show up. In the quiet all that could be heard was the rustling of the leaves and the birdsongs carried on the breeze. Shielding my eyes from the brilliant sunshine, I stared at the cloudless blue sky listening to the soothing voice of Mother Nature.

A little while later another canoe finally showed up. "Where is everyone," my brother asked.

"We're the only ones coming," said Dennis, "The others gave up when they saw the chute."

Our group of ten was now down to four people and two canoes. We made plans to stick together for the remainder of the trip just in case there were any more mishaps.

My brother got lunch ready while I reflected on the familiar history of the mighty river. My father had fished this river all his life as did his father and grandfather before him. It was amazing to be in a place that had been such an important part of my father's life. I was recalling some of his fishing stories about the big salmon that were caught here and of course the bigger ones that got away, when to my complete surprise a salmon jumped out of the water right in front of me. "Life just doesn't get any better than this", I whispered.

After lunch, we picked up every single thing we brought with us so as not to leave a footprint in the pristine environment. From my perch in the bow of the canoe I marveled at how clean the forest was along the riverbank. We moved silently along and every once in a while a salmon leapt out of the water, glistening silver in the mid-afternoon sun. This is what it's all about, I thought. I was in a transcended state of mind, and I didn't want the trip to end. Then my brother said, "Okay we've got one more chute coming up in a little bit, but it's not as big as the last one." In the heat of the summer day I was suddenly chilled to the bone.

"What exactly do you mean by not as big?" I asked. "Never mind, just let me know when we get there because I'm getting out of the canoe. I'll meet you at the bottom of the chute."

My brother laughed, but promised to tell me when we got closer. It was about half an hour later when the mood of the river changed again. I could hear the hiss and knew what was coming so we stopped a short distance from the top of the chute and I waded to the shore in the fast-moving thigh deep water.

My brother waited until I had picked my way to the bottom of the drop along the rocky riverbank before he started through the chute. It wasn't much of a drop and he skillfully guided the canoe over the edge landing with a gentle splash in the pool below. The canoe behind him also navigated the chute without a problem and I felt kind of silly passing on the ride, but the huge black and blue bumps on my legs, arms and head were solemn reminders of the nightmare chute number one had been.

A short time later we came upon a fairly deep salmon pool. The water was warm and inviting and crystal clear. Deciding this would be a great chance to swim and take a break before we finished our trip we jumped in. It was exhilarating. Although it was impossible to swim against the current, it was fun to be carried through the pool with no effort whatsoever and we played like children for the better part of an hour. I felt at peace with myself and with everything around me.

Afterward we finished off the rest of the sandwiches, and then exhausted - yet elated - I thought how awesome it would be to do this again someday. My legs were throbbing, my arms ached from exertion, but the adrenalin rush was in high gear. Next time I'd be better equipped to handle whatever came my way.

Back in the canoe we continued our trek. The river was wider now and seemed a lot faster. My brother said, "Better start rowing harder now. We want to get straight through without going sideways."

I began rowing with everything I had, beads of sweat rolling down my face with the exertion. I'd inquire about the perils of going sideways later, for now I just wanted to do my part to get us though. My muscles screamed for me to give up but I didn't want us going sideways so I paddled harder and harder. In a little while the water grew calm and we glided smoothly into another salmon pool. I glanced around to ask my brother if it was okay to stop rowing, and I couldn't believe my eyes! There he sat, reclining against the back of the canoe with his legs stretched out and a silly grin on his face. I realized he'd been relaxing the entire time I'd been paddling like a mad woman.

At my indignant look he burst into gales of laughter and to my surprise I did too. With tears of laughter streaming down my cheeks, I simply had to ask, "Exactly how many times during this trip did you make me row like the devil was chasing us while you sat back and enjoyed the ride? Never mind, don't tell me because if I could summon the strength I'd hit you with this oar."

The sun was sinking low in the sky and the enormity of the day was rapidly catching up with me when we finally rounded the last bend. My entire body was in agony and I realized I couldn't have done another five minutes in that canoe. When we pulled ashore my brother wrapped me in a big bear hug.

"You're a real trooper Sis; you did it. Now go on home and get some rest. I'll take care of everything here."

Before the trip I thought I was in great physical condition. But as I stood there in the hot shower counting my bumps and bruises I realized

I'd used muscles I had no idea I owned. I'd never been so physically exhausted in my life.

The hot water was soothing; and as I thought about the places I'd been that day, I began feeling extraordinarily emotional. Then right out of the blue uncontrollable sobs wracked my body as I sank to the shower floor. The exhilaration of taking on nature and feeling so deeply connected to the earth and then leaving it all behind had left me with a lonely ache in my heart. In that moment I wished I was back on the river in the middle of nowhere, where everything was in perfect harmony.

Miss Adventure I'm not, but the sense of euphoria at having felt nature's heartbeat right next to mine far outweighed every trial I endured on that twenty-two-kilometer learning curve. I carried away a wealth of life lessons and earned an even deeper respect for the awesome power and beauty of nature.

Would I do it again? I'm sixty years old now, so the opportunity won't likely present itself at this point in my life. However, I'll carry the blissful memories of those twenty-two kilometers with me forever.

About Annabel:

Annabel Sheila grew up beside beautiful Bay St. George in picturesque Stephenville, Newfoundland. Eternally inspired to write about nature, the ocean, love and life she happily embraces her muse's gentle nudge.

Displaced Marvels

By

JoeAnn Hart

Have you been to the beach today?" Caroline asked.

"There's the oddest animal by the boathouse steps. Run down before the tide takes it away."

Caroline's call came in the aftermath of a late winter storm off the Atlantic, a long arm of a beast that had swept out to sea then curved back to hit us like a fist. The gale blew for seventy hours and battered the earth with rain. Now that it was over and the wind had died, I could hear the ocean continue to pound the beach like a war drum.

"Is it dead or alive?" I asked, wondering whether to bring a camera or a cage.

"Oh, it's quite dead," she said. "If not, we're in trouble. I've never seen anything like it!"

I couldn't wait. I am one for whom the words "gruesome discovery" on the evening news makes me turn up the volume. Caroline is over eighty and has lived on the beach for sixty years, so if something washed up that she couldn't identify, it had to be good. Maybe it could even be as good as the giant squid in recent headlines. Japanese scientists in a submarine dove down to the sunless world where the cephalopod lived and took the first ever photograph of its living, undulant, self. Before that, its existence was known only in myth or in death, when a fifty-foot carcass might wash ashore to the horror of the locals. They would then proceed to eat it. Perhaps this mystery creature on the beach would be my giant squid, something revealed only to a special few. We are so physically and psychologically remote from what goes on in the aquatic world. It was not inconceivable that a storm of this magnitude could dislodge such a beast. Sometimes it takes turmoil and chaos to bring something up from the darkness.

I grabbed my camera and called my dog, Daisy, to help me find whatever it was I was looking for, and headed to the beach path. My mind was awash with exotic possibilities. The ocean's inhabitants are stranger than we think, and sometimes stranger than we are even able to conceive. Think of the Yeti Crab, with its tiny body and huge hairy arms. It was discovered only in 2005, next to a 700 degree hydrothermal vent near the Easter Islands, where the surrounding waters are just above freezing. Pure white, and as its name suggests, looking more like a baby Abominable Snowman than a crab, it would be quite a sight on our Massachusetts beach. So would an Ocean sunfish, a member of the violent and dangerous Pufferfish family, which can grow ten feet across with a brain the size of a hazelnut. It looks like a disembodied head with fins and frills in all the wrong places. They are seen in New England coastal waters, so Caroline would be familiar with one in its natural habitat, floating on the surface, enticing seabirds to feast on its parasites. However, splayed out on the beach, it would be a wet rubber rug with eyes. Then there is the Nudibranch tribe, mollusks who gave up their shells eons ago, opting instead for toxicity and wild coloring to keep predators at bay. They are stunning pieces of designer fabric pulsing in the water, but washed up; they would look like a mass execution of clowns.

The sky was seal-gray, and I could smell the groin scented beach before I got there. The storm tide-line was half-way up the path, thirty feet above normal, and I had to climb over hummocks of seaweed and kick aside splintered planks. I paused at the entrance of the beach while Daisy ran ahead to worry the seagulls, who rose a few feet in the air at her approach, then settled back down with a laugh. They were overjoyed with the beachcomber's meaty abundance and refused to be moved along by the likes of Daisy. It was a loud and active scene. The face of the water was still angry. The rising tide seethed around the rocks, churning the seaweed and marine debris at the waterline. Swells continued to push sand and rocks ashore, and it seemed as if the whole beach had shifted to the right. Ignoring the grim significance of white feathers littering the length of the cove, the gulls hopped over smashed building materials, delighting in every storm-damaged mussel or limp jellyfish without the usual squabbling over rights. They picked through piles of indigestible plastic disgorged by the sea, the net balls of tangled line, the water bottles, the blue rubber gloves that are the standard issue of the fishing fleet, which, when beached, are like hands reaching up from the grave. *The sea tosses up our losses*, as T.S. Elliot says, (*The Dry Salvages*, Four Quartets, Harcourt 1943) who summered in his youth not far from the spot where I stood.

As I maneuvered the shore, there was so much to take in, natural and otherwise, that I passed Caroline's creature twice before my brain caught up to my eyes. It was not a whole animal. It was only a head, come to rest on a bier of seaweed: A mammalian head, vaguely Hobbit-like, with a long, naked snout and thick furry ears. But whose? Daisy sat at my feet, staring but not investigating. She was keeping her distance, and I knew she knew. What animal did she avoid?

"Coyote," I said out loud. It was the head of a coyote. Unexpected, certainly, disturbing by any accounts, but a giant squid it was not. It didn't even call the sea home, but I could see why Caroline was freaked out. It was a freakish thing. Where the fur had been eaten away was now a pinkish-white sheen, making the face human. The pale, pupil-less eyes were eerie and watchful, their lids having been nibbled off by fish. A collar of seaweed was draped across a withered stump of a neck, whose exposed flesh was pickled by the brine. What was so surprising, aside from the fact that a chunk of woodland animal had been coughed up by the sea, was that there was any flesh left at all- or bone. The sea is usually more efficient than that. An environmentally correct funeral would be to put a body in a crab pool, and a few days later – poof! -- no more body. The storm must have disrupted this particular death banquet.

I listened to the water hitting the seaweed-slick rocks. This was a dangerous place. Coyotes scavenge the shoreline, but they're not stupid. It seemed unlikely one would have been out in the storm. Maybe it had gone out beforehand and was snared by a rogue wave that snapped it in two. Huge timbers had been hauled up in pieces, why not a fragile body? But my gut told me he'd been killed by a human and tossed unceremoniously into the brink, where fish and waves had begun to make quick work of a dirty job. The animal was no undiscovered marvel of the natural world, but a monster of our own making thrown back at us.

From the paw prints in the sand I could see that dogs, like my Daisy, had already come by and had left the coyote unmolested, whether from fear or affinity to the pack. I stroked the fur lightly on his forehead, then I left him alone. The sea would take care of him. It was voracious. Let the currents break him up into meal. Let him unite with his body to become whole again. I shot some photos and I said a prayer.

> *May we all come together in this place*
> *where the land meets the sea,*
> *like body and soul,*
> *which reveals our deepest secrets*
> *and exposes our fears, and then*
> *let us leave it in peace.*

Daisy and I headed back to the house with the tide creeping up behind us. I was not there when the coyote rolled back into the water, but I imagined the moment, in the green gloom of the sea, when he is discovered. Fish begin circling around him; crabs scuttle over, everyone curious about this unknown being, which sets them pondering the great mysteries of the terrestrial world, before tucking in for the feast.

About JoeAnn:

JoeAnn Hart is the author of the novels Float *and* Addled, *fiction with a social conscience. Her short fiction, essays, and articles have been widely published.*

Note: This essay originally appeared in The Little Patuxent Review, Issue 15, Winter 2014.

Swimming the Sea

By

Kim Powell

There is something incredibly intoxicating about the smell of freshly digested anchovies. A chemical cue signals to the olfactory portion of our brain that an exuberant humpback whale *(Megaptera novaeangliae)* is nearby. As a baleen whale surfaces, a blast of hot air explodes out through a pair of blowholes forming a unique signature. A heart shaped spout reveals that a gray whale *(Eschrichitius robustus)* is nearby, likely on its incredible journey between Alaska and the lagoons of Baja, Mexico. A spout rocketing 30 feet in the air indicates that the largest species on earth, the blue whale *(Balaenoptera musculus)* has made an appearance.

Sitting in a sea kayak in Monterey Bay, an oily mist of anchovy breath suddenly saturated our senses. Hearts pounding, we quickly backed up, as a humpback whale surfaced.

It was my friend Karen's birthday and as promised I had taken her kayaking in Monterey Bay National Marine Sanctuary. Coined the "Serengeti of the Sea" Monterey Bay harbors 34 species of marine mammals making it a premier whale-watching destination. From the shore we had noticed a concentration of both seas birds and sea lions indicating that humpback whales may be feeding below them. We soon found ourselves surrounded by a pod of very energetic and enthusiastic sea lions *(Zalophus californianus)*. A male sea lion can exceed 8 feet in length and weigh 800 pounds. When a posy of seal lions takes to the air in a behavior known as porpoising, it grabs your attention. Gaining greater speed while airborne, sea lions improve their hunting skills. They may also porpoise to avoid the advances of a predator, namely an orca (*Orcinus orca*) or white shark (*Carcharodon carcharias*). The prey in this case were the anchovies which were feeding on a rich soup of plankton.

As the sea lions rocketed towards us, our immediate response was to back paddle. Instinctively, we started tapping our plastic vessel, sending out an aquatic Morse code to any large mammal that might be below us. Moments later, one of the most profound encounters of my career as a naturalist occurred. But this was not my first oceanic encounter.

On a sultry summer day in July, 1969, I saw my first marine mammal, a West Indian manatee (*Trichechus manatus*). Later that day, I would discover a sooty sea hare, (*Aplysia brasiliana*), a slimy marine invertebrate washed ashore on a gulf beach. Although I was only 11 years old at the time, these discoveries spoke to me. My life long passion for exploring blue waters had begun.

My father and I had a weekend tradition during that first summer in Florida. We would head out into emerald hues of the Gulf of Mexico and throw in a fishing line. It was our time to marvel together at the ecological wonders of our new salty home. Fishing in Florida was quite different from the creeks of my childhood in Ohio.

In Florida, Dad and I stood waist deep in the warm gulf water, when suddenly, something was bobbing near us in the murky sea; something dark and rotund emerged next to us. It was breathing through what appeared to be hairy nostrils and gazed up at us through tiny dark eyes. . My dad was a big man with a commanding personality, yet his eyes were unblinking and wide as he stumbled backwards. He then shrieked. It was a sound quite unfamiliar to my 11-year-old ears. A manatee had visited us.

For centuries, the sailors who first encountered manatees thought they were part woman and part fish - seductive fair maidens of the sea. Living a fully aquatic life, these 2000-pound herbivores are members of a group of marine mammals known as the Sirenians.

Manatees are gentle, slow moving mammals that are now endangered throughout their range. Boat strikes, marine debris and habitat loss have taken their toll on these lumbering gentle giants of the sea. Planet earth will lose one of its most benevolent creatures if the manatee, due to human recklessness, is forced to extinction.

Tragically, the largest fish on our planet the whale shark (*Rhincodon typus*) has been depleted, their dorsal fins harvested for the shark fin soup industry. (If you ever see Tofu shark listed on a menu, please consider another option.) Whale sharks display an exotic design of white spots draped across a dark body, which can reach 60 feet in length. After clocking in 100's of hours of night snorkeling in the Caribbean, I had rarely encountered a shark. But before one dips into the inky darkness of tropical waters the question of shark encounters arises.

Spotting a 30 foot shark, a group of fearless women - on our first expedition to swim in the waters of Baja – donned their masks, snorkel and fins. We sat teetering on the edge of our skiff, legs dangling and our derrieres finding that delicate balance between comfort and pain; and we waited for the command. An excited voiced bellowed "Ok, Ok, Si Si go now, go now". The command echoed across the water and without hesitation ker-plunk went our derrieres.

There is something mildly counterintuitive when ker-plunking into murky water where a shark is known to be. Across the waves, I could hear my co-leader, Andra Farstad's elevated voice proclaim, "Remember to swim away from the mouth".

As with any large aquatic animal it is always best to swim parallel to a species. This particular shark with a massive mouth quite capable of devouring a delicate lady leg, had a different agenda. The shark slowly turned its head toward one of the women, with a mouth gaping open as it filtered plankton from the water. Back on the boat with all limbs accounted for, a group of women were united by a shared and sublime experience.

Back with my friend Karen, in the anchovy waters of Monterey Bay, we continued our tapping. As we drifted and tapped, a humpback whale silently raised its rostrum (head region) out of the water approximately four feet from us. This astounding behavior is known as "spy hopping", when a whale approaches an object such as a boat to take a better look. Karen turned at that precise moment, her eyes meeting the curious stare of an 80,000-pound creature; a birthday gift that she will never forget.

As quietly as it had arrived, the stealthy whale sunk back below the water line without making a ripple. Every pore of my body was acutely aware as adrenaline pulsated through me. Humbled, honored, inspired and in awe we paddled back to shore. Once again, my life had been deeply enriched by an extraordinary encounter with an incredible species of the sea.

About Kim:

Kim Powell is owner, operator and naturalist at Blue Water Ventures in Santa Cruz, CA. Her business offers naturalist-led field trips for students and adventurous vacations for adults designed to be relaxing and educational. Living on the edge of Monterey Bay National Marine Sanctuary, Kim has been organizing excursions to extraordinarily beautiful places since 1985. Kim enjoys watching marine wildlife while kayaking, snorkeling, surfing and boogie boarding.

Pug Boat

By

Rebecca Lawton

When the Water Rat in *Wind in the Willows* expressed the universal truth that "there is *nothing*—absolutely nothing—half so much worth doing as simply messing about in boats," he didn't mention that those who mess about long enough will someday find themselves out of the boat. They'll land in the water, and, to again quote the Rat, they'll be living "by it and with it and on it and in it."

Certainly I have gone in the drink, usually without the boat going over. "As if you'd jumped," observed a friend who once filmed my unplanned plummet from the helm of a 22-foot rubber raft I was rowing through Lava Falls, one of the most difficult regularly navigated rapids in America.

My boat did not go over on that trip—it hovered on an end tube and pitched me and no one else—or on any other during the ten seasons I guided in the Grand Canyon. But I did swim the rapids of the Colorado River more than once, with just my head and shoulders above the roiling mountains of muddy waves. I survived by reminding myself to breathe air and not swallow water in the midst of it. And I got good at messing about both in and out of boats.

No one loved hearing about my periodic misadventures half so much as my daughter Rose. From the moment she could form a sentence, she was hungry for words and beyond her years in verbal ability. "Tell me a bedtime story, Mom," she'd say, gazing up from her pillow.

"What kind? About dinosaurs?" I'd ask. The giant lizards were another favorite topic.

. "Tell me about Pug."

Pug was the family dinghy. It was a wooden El Toro built by my father the same year I was born. He'd christened it with a nickname he'd also given my mother. Pug was an integral part of the summers I spent with my parents and my three siblings at Clear Lake, the largest natural lake entirely within California.

Our beloved summer place was ridiculed by schoolmates who preferred the more highbrow Lake Tahoe. Clear Lake was a bit of a backwater. The wooden porch of the grocery store gathered ne'er-do-wells we had to circumvent to reach the racks of comic books inside. The ramshackle resorts along the lakeshore were unlike the fancy hotels of Tahoe's South Shore. And in truth Clear Lake wasn't very clear. Rachel Carson wrote of it in *Silent Spring*, "The name is plainly inappropriate; actually, the lake is rather turbid, because its bottom, which is shallow, is covered with soft black ooze." She went on to describe how enormous quantities of pesticides applied to control gnats in the 1950s led to the die-off of Western grebes and other birds around the lake. We who grew up sailing, swimming, and fishing there were hardly aware of gnats or poisons, and apparently our parents hadn't learned about them either.

At Clear Lake we also lived with a pervasive algae that edged the shores in green muck and stunk like a reeking pile of dead weeds. Fortunately, a sailboat or rowboat launched quickly escaped the guck and emerged onto an open expanse of naturally warm water. Pug, built for one but sometimes piled into by two or three of us, facilitated our flight from shore.

Rose, sensing my passion for the place and the boat, would ask at bedtime, "Tell me about when you had to be rescued in Pug."

"When Grandpa sent me out on my own and I couldn't get back to the dock?"

"Uh-huh. That one."

"Okay. Once upon a time, when I was eight years old, Grandpa thought I was ready to sail Pug by myself."

"But you couldn't."

"Right. I sailed a short way out and didn't know how to turn around.

So I sat and screamed."

"And the motorboats had to come out and get you."

"Well, Grandpa was coming out in the bigger sailboat. His Thistle."

"But he was too slow."

"I'm sure he would have gotten there in time to help me."

"But the motorboats saved you first."

"Right. There were two of them so they had to decide who would pull me to shore."

Rose thought a moment. "But you survived it," she said, using one of our favorite expressions.

"Right. I learned to sail Pug everywhere—down the lake to town, across to Wilson's Beach with Aunt Jen, out to Rattlesnake Island—"

"Have I ever been to Rattlesnake Island?"

"No. You can't land there anymore. Somebody owns it. And there are Native Americans whose great grandmothers and grandfathers are buried there. They don't want anyone disturbing them. Anyway, good night. They all lived happily ever after."

Rattlesnake Island, although off limits to Rose and me, still captured our imaginations. Its shores beckoned while battles raged about the ownership of its fifty-seven remote and wild acres and what to do about the ancient burial grounds mid island. And in the 1950s and 1960s, before any such controversy came to light, my siblings and I had landed Pug and a battered old rowboat there to explore. Signs of excavation and heaped soil gave us the creeps, so we often ran back to the boats and launched on the fly. On one of these fleet-footed escapes, my younger brother and I leapt over a deer carcass being ravaged by yellow jackets. They swarmed after us, stinging us dozens of times. We reported back to our parents with welts and tears, and I hadn't been back to the island since.

About thirty years after the rescue by motorboats and attack by yellowjackets, I'd inherited Pug. I'd repaired her lines and slapped on fresh paint. Sometimes I threw her on the roof of my station wagon to take Rose camping at Clear Lake. We'd pitch our tent on the west shore, day sail, read books, and generally enjoy lake living. Rose became so used to riding in the bow of Pug on those trips that she invariably dozed off, lulled by the breezes and waves.

One late summer day, I drove Pug to Clear Lake. I planned to circumnavigate Rattlesnake Island alone. In my imagination, the owners or occupants would beckon me ashore to old haunts that were now (I hoped) receiving the respect they deserved. When I arrived, Clear Lake looked as sparkling as ever, with the great sleeping volcano Mount Konocti on the west shore and the dusty green of oak forests climbing the hills. Leaves on buckeyes and big-leaf maples fluttered burnt orange and yellow in onshore breezes. Gray pines gleamed silver in the sunlight. Beyond the boat ramp where I launched into a small bay, healthy morning breezes would carry me to Rattlesnake in no time. Pug's tiller, centerboard, and lines were as familiar to me as if I'd never been away.

As I sailed on, the breezes built to a hard blow. This, too, was familiar, as I remembered how wind whipped the water into whitecaps nearly every afternoon. Swells rolled down lake in rough formation. Pug began to feel small out there, tossed and slapped by curlers. I sailed for three hours, tacking and coming about on a determined trajectory for Rattlesnake. But I was making scant headway, and I noticed other boats returning to dock.

A series of scares told me it was time to head back, also: first, I almost washed onto a beach where a lakeside owner shouted something I couldn't hear (and perhaps didn't want to) before I turned Pug about and sailed off. Then I came within inches of ramming a group of buoys that warned of dangerous shallows that could shear off Pug's centerboard. Next, I swept too close to black, rocky shoals, not once, but twice. Island or no island, it was time to get out of there.

I'd have to fall off the wind and head down lake. I was at least a mile from the dock. Timing was of the essence in turning downwind. If done as a swell washed toward Pug's stern, she'd be swamped. I did have oars and I could lower the sails and row for it. I would try that next.

As gradually as the gales would allow, I came about. Pug swung parallel with the swells just as one washed up and over her little stern. Shifting my weight forward, I was too slow. Another larger swell washed in and filled the cockpit. Bless her little wooden heart, Pug sunk in slow motion before capsizing. I was able to keep my wits and gather all my gear as we went over. I grabbed the hull, pulled the mast and boom to the surface, and held them all together. I had a couple of choices: stick with the boat and wait for rescue, or swim for the nearest shore, probably a quarter mile away.

The only thing that deterred me from taking off swimming was the lake traffic—sleek, low-profile bass boats had been criss crossing the water all day. Swimmers were fairly invisible to the fast-moving boats in whitecaps. Just as I made up my mind to risk it, drop everything, and swim, a bass boat roared over to investigate my flotsam.

They pulled up beside me and shut off their motor. Two men in fishing caps and vests leaned over the side and gazed down from their blue lamé speedboat.

"You're in a heck of a predicament," said one.

The other nodded, but only for a moment before getting to work lifting first me, then Pug mast and all onto his fiberglass deck. The fishermen also gathered up my mast, boom, oars, cooler with snacks, tiller, rudder, and centerboard. Wrapping me in a blanket, they sped me back to the dock.

Onshore, their fishing buddies were waiting with beers in hand. "Sam, you've been fishing for three days and all you can catch is an El Toro and a mermaid?"

They helped me load Pug onto my wagon and said good-bye. I drove off, not injured except for pride, and remembered Rattlesnake. If I wasn't going to get within sailing distance, the least I could do was take a gander from shore. I passed homes and docks, old bait stores, marine fueling stations, small coves where ducks lay tucked in from the wind, and clusters of sailboats pulled ashore. The paved road soon looped around a point. Then I saw it: huge, verdant, and empty. Rattlesnake looked misty with spray, its irregular shoreline pounded by waves. Through binoculars I stared at the lush thickness of the woods and varicolored lichens on boulders that lined the water. It was still the mysterious destination that would make for good bedtime stories.

I knew I'd have some explaining to do when I made my usual phone call to Rose that night.

"What took you so long, Mom?" she asked.

"I was out sailing today. And I tipped over!"

"In Pug?"

"Yeah. Right in the middle of Clear Lake. I was trying to sail around Rattlesnake Island, and I went over, lunch bucket and all."

"But you survived it?" she asked.

"Yeah. A motorboat came along just in time to pick me up."

"The motorboats saved you again?"

"Well, just one this time. A fishing boat. They said they'd caught a mermaid!"

"Did they really think you were one?"

"No, they were just teasing. But it's too bad I didn't get close to Rattlesnake. It looks like somewhere Peter Pan would live."

"Wow! Can we sail around it sometime?"

"Of course. In a bigger sailboat. Sleep tight tonight, sweetie. They all lived happily ever after."

About Rebecca:

Rebecca Lawton's debut novel, Junction, Utah, *is based on her life as a Western river guide (van Haitsma, 2013). Her collaboration with photographer Geoff Fricker,* Sacrament: Homage to a River, *was published by Heyday (2014). Her book of essays,* Reading Water *(2003), was a San Francisco Chronicle bestseller.*

Silently Canoeing

By

Kelly Williams

I grew up in Ontario's cottage country. My childhood was filled with playing in the forest, swimming in the river, and climbing trees. Every family leisure activity was done outside. We boated in the summer and snowmobiled in the winter. The spring was the ideal play time because our little tar and gravel dead-end road produced shallow gullies running down the sides that formed small rivers when the snow started to melt. That's when the neighborhood kids came out to race toothpicks and cheer their tiny sticks through the micro rapids. Nature was the backdrop for all the playing and adventuring that happened with my friends and family.

When I was a teen, however, I learned that Mother Nature had even more to offer - solitude. After school, I eased our dirty white canoe into the water and set off. I paddled through the lily pads on my way to the spot where my dad took me fishing. There, I would watch the sun fish dart around and poke at sunken timbers-the last reminders of the lumber mill that once stood where the dam is now. I wasn't thinking about homework or friend drama. I was looking for turtles and crayfish and listening to frogs call to one another. My mind wasn't turned off, it was tuned in, and I liked it. I didn't know what to call it then, but now I see I was living in the moment. I was all alone but not lonely in the least.

After high school, a full decade passed without much nature in my life. I was living in the city where solitude in nature was a distant sentiment.

Private outdoor space was in the form of a concrete balcony. I did face the CN Tower though, and loved watching the lightning strike it when a thunderstorm rolled through. I would walk in my neighborhood and enjoy the old growth trees, but they weren't mine. I wasn't allowed to try to climb them, and they were too close to the road to comfortably park there with a book. When I went home to visit, I would soak up my surroundings like a sponge so I could take that sense of peace back with me to the bustling, loud city.

When I moved to the suburbs, I thought a yard might be enough to satisfy my need to be outside. Sadly this wasn't the case. The houses were practically built on top of one another and the yard was about the size of a postage stamp. But the size of the yard wasn't the main problem; the main problem there was nothing to do outside. No exploring, no wildlife to spy, no trees to climb, not even a garden to tend.

A garden had been on my mind, but my fiancée and I couldn't agree on what we wanted. I forced a small garden on him just before we got married because we were having a party the day after our wedding and the back yard needed some sprucing up. It was pretty sad to be honest, but I loved my mini rosebushes, tiger lilies, and petunias. I needed more though. It was years later that I finally convinced my husband to help me make a big garden in the front of our house. Big is a relative term, but compared to what I had, this new garden was a large slice of heaven. I could fill hours weeding, watering, and caring for my plants. It's the closest I'd come to finding the feeling I had in my canoe.

When I'm out in the garden I'm not making mental to-do lists or thinking about what I need to make for dinner. I don't even listen to music. I go out and see what needs to be done and I do it. That's all I'm thinking about, what I'm doing at that given moment. I don't know if other people will understand what a huge gift that is, to not think about a dozen things, but it is. When I'm finished in the garden I don't have the sense of pride I have when I complete other tasks. It's more of a feeling of gratitude. I'm thankful that I've had the time to just be and I'm thankful that nature stands still for no one and that I will have to do it all again very soon.

I still love going back to my little home town. My garden is like a sip of water on a hot day, but my home town is a pitcher full of icy satisfaction. When I go there now, I drive around looking for properties for sale. The likelihood of my buying a cottage is slim to none, but I can dream. I can dream about toothpick races, and sunfish, listening to frogs, and sitting alone in a canoe. I can dream and not think.

About Kelly:

Kelly Williams is a former technical writer, current freelance writer, and mom to four. She's working on her third degree black belt and eating humble pie in the process. She translates her karate lessons into life lessons, helping her become a better person and parent.
Twitter: @KellyWilli
Blogs BlackBeltMommy.wordpress.com and
KellyWilli.wordpress.com

Felling a Friend

By

Roslyn Imrie

My best friend died in the wicked frost of April 2006.

On April 16th it snowed. Blushing from early spring, the dogwood flowers, red buds, and apple blossoms wore frosty cocoons. In Arkansas, it seldom snows in March, not to mention April. For three days, the high was 17 degrees Fahrenheit. The following week did not see temperatures above freezing. Fruit trees throughout the Ozarks did not produce the following fall. Many trees died, including my red oak tree; my best friend.

As a child, I had very few friends. Well, human friends anyway. My closest friends were trees. In the Boston Mountains of the Ozarks, trees are bountiful and diverse. For endless hours, I climbed trees or basked in their shade. I knew many soft spoken cedars, lofty pines, broad-leafed hickories, prickly sweet gums, ghostly beeches, and outstretched oaks.

Among them, I cherished an old red oak the most. She boldly stood about ten feet from the front porch with a wide, symmetric canopy, supported by huge branches. It was perfect for a swing, which my father hung over the driveway from her lowest branch. I loved that swing.

I would leap off the porch, swing out over the driveway, past the staghorn sumac, above the flowering dogwood, until my toes touched the low-hanging hickory branches beyond. I sat, for a moment, suspended at the pinnacle of the pendulum, reaching for the sky.

The inevitable force of gravity pulled me away from the hickory canopies, the flowering dogwoods, past the staghorn sumac, back over the driveway, and as I leaned backwards as far as I could, my long blonde ponytail would lick the roof of the log cabin my father built.

Swing out, pause, and swing back.

Summers crept past as I swung in the tree's growing shade. The tree's dark shadows, which kept the yard devoid of weeds, began to cast over her lower branches. One summer, while swinging, I looked up at the branch my swing hung from to see it naked. I realized the swinging limb was dead. My father simply moved the swing to another branch. But soon that limb also died. While the tree's health dwindled, I grew out of my childish ways and explored other means of reaching for the sky.

After the April freeze, none of her leaves returned. I waited all summer for those leaves. In fall, I pretended she wasn't dead, but only naked from the winter's chill. But when spring returned, and her leaves did not, I knew there was no hope. She was deceased.

Though the tree obviously threatened the house, it took me two years to cut her down. For one thing, I was afraid to fell a tree so close to the house. But more importantly, cutting her down was like pulling the plug on my grandmother. She stood tall and beautiful, even as a skeleton. Soon her brittle fingers began to splinter and break, scattering twigs about the yard. In fall, after hurricane Ike, a large branch fell on the house. It tore off only one shingle and we repaired it with ease, but I took it as a solemn warning. I couldn't bear the thought of the tree crushing the house my father built with his own hands, the house I grew up in, my home. We prepared to cut her down.

We gathered the necessary materials: two chainsaws, plenty of bar oil and gasoline, a thick chain, a long ladder, and a 4X4 Ford truck with a winch on its bumper. My father started by climbing the ladder and swinging a chain around the tree's trunk about 20 feet up, where he looped it around her lowest branch. Then he hooked the chain to the winch. The truck was parked about 100 feet away, where the tree's limbs couldn't reach it. We chained the truck's back bumper to another tree to anchor it. With all this in place we began cutting, cautiously. Logic told us she would want to fall to the north since the land leaned that way. The truck's winch, to the west, would keep her from falling east- onto the house.

The first cut was a wedge in the north side of the tree. As his saw sunk into her trunk, the pungent aroma of oak flooded my nose. I wanted to stop him. I had to remind myself that she was already dead. But then, when he removed the wedge of wood from the tree, she began to bleed. From her heartwood, a stream of water began to squirt, as if we had hit an artery. I tenderly touched the wet heartwood, expecting a pulse. She was warm.

My father explained that some of the tree's branches must have been partly hollow and full of water. The pressurized water was draining through her core, causing the bleeding. Her warmth was explained away by the friction of the chainsaw blade.

After she stopped bleeding, my father began cutting into the opposite side of the trunk. As he cut, he stuck wedges he had made from 2X4s into his cut so the tree wouldn't pinch his saw blade. The wedges would also encourage the tree to fall in the desired direction.

This continued tediously as the sun sunk below the tree line and then below the mountains in the distance. *Any second now*, we kept thinking. All the while we ran from one side of the tree to the other, expecting the tree to fall at any time, but not knowing which way she would fall. At last, there was nothing but a pie-sized sliver holding her massive body erect.

Why wouldn't she fall? Why did she lean towards the house? Did she want to destroy the house? Maybe for all these years she had dreamed of falling on the house and crushing it with one fell blow. Her massive trunk may have wanted to splinter the red oak logs that made up our humble home. Perhaps she wanted to take us with her. Maybe it was some type of revenge for cutting the nearby oak trees in the building of the house.

"It really wants to fall on the house," my father said. "The winch must be holding it up."

"But it looks so symmetrical," I said.

"The branches away from the house, must be hollow. It must be weighted over the house."

"Please don't let it fall on the house, Papa."

"I don't think it will. It may take out the greenhouse or the far corner of the porch though."

"It's getting dark."

"Maybe if I pull on the winch."

My father returned to the truck and tried pulling on the winch. The winch strained, but the tree held fast. Then he flicked the switch and loosed the winch cable. Immediately, the tree began to fall towards the house. I screamed. Quickly, my father reversed the winch.

The tree began to swing. She swung back, paused, and swung out. She licked the roof of the log cabin my father built with her long bare branches. She balanced for a moment at the pinnacle of the pendulum, reaching for the sky one last time. Then the inevitable force of gravity pulled her down and away from the cabin. Swinging out over the driveway, crushing the staghorn sumac, splintering the flowering dogwood, and breaking those low-hanging hickory branches beyond, she fell.

About Roslyn:

Roslyn Imrie is a writer, mother, and teacher who grew up in the Ozark Mountains, close to the earth, in a log cabin - without running water or electricity. She currently lives near the region of her childhood , where she raises two boys, tends a garden, nurtures an orchard, and cares for chickens.

Wildlife Friends

By

Mary Nida Smith

When I moved to places I didn't want to be and found myself very lonely, God sent his creatures that roam the earth without fences to find and befriend me. Their contact with me made me feel loved. It started with an extra lot next to our property we had purchased when we moved into Devonshire Subdivision in a small town of 700, in the natural state of Arkansas. We were surrounded by woods. The lot - a third of an acre of overgrown vines, bushes and trees - had to be cleared just enough to remove the poison ivy and create a habitat for me and my new found friends. Of course I wanted to beautify it for me, my feathered friends and for all the creatures that enjoyed a little color. I planted bushes, flowers and vines on and around the deck. With a camera in hand, was when I first noticed a full-grown gray-colored tree frog inside a small layered flower pot. This one - or a different one - returned every year and then one evening it all changed.

A gray colored tree frog the size of the end of a pencil I named Sassafras (Sass) entered my life hanging on the side of a small bird bath on the deck railing. I was excited to see one so tiny. The next morning I captured a photo of Sass leaning over the rim of a large flower saucer. Later it moved to the patio table into a log bird house, where it sunbathed, cooled its body in a flower pot saucer of water, and adventured out at dusk allowing me to capture many photographs.

The following year Sass moved up front under the three large oaks and a hickory tree. After he moved, large red wasps moved into the bird house, allowing me to learn about their family. Each year I continue to make new summer friends. We have conversations as I speak softly with a, "Hi, how are you today?" Mrs. M. and her other squirrel friends will cry out high in the trees to warn me there is danger nearby – the stray cat. They will look in the direction they see danger. I continue to speak softly to reassure Mrs. M. and her friends while I search and remove the cat from the area. Yapping with joy, they all run down the trees toward the sunflower seeds. They also remind me when they need food, water, a dust hole to roll in, or soft soil to plant nuts in. I have learned from a skinny fox, a fat winterized groundhog, many seasonal deer families, (I can speak their language and stomp my feet with the best of them), a skink, spiders, chipmunks, turtles, birds, snakes, , frogs and insects.

One late afternoon as I searched the woodland garden from my window, I finally spotted the small, motherless fawn I had been feeding named Prissy. For about three days, she stopped coming by until that evening. I called, "Prissy, Prissy", she looked up, came toward me as I spoke softly to her. She stopped below the open window, looked up at me, smelled her corn, then turned back to the woods. She did this twice, and then she disappeared into and out of the woods. I was so happy to know she was okay, except for missing spots of fur. I love talking to the animals. They understand what I am saying more than most people.

One summer my buddy was an Orb garden spider that peeked in my bedroom window and I stared back. She allowed me to snap pictures and write a children's story about her in free verse. As we started to become friends, she decided to stay to teach me about web building. That she did, spinning the width and length of the window. Over the years her relatives have shared their talents. I enjoyed photographing one spinning a line from a corner of the house to the morning glory vine trellis alongside the herb garden and seeing how it surprised its prey.

I continue to meet new friends and photograph them. I even save insects that fall into the large birdbath and are having difficulty swimming to the edge.. Most insects can only dog paddle. And, I must not forget my family of titmice that moved into the second bird house near where Sass use to live. The Titmice allowed me to become their friend and to watch them through the patio window building their nest and raising their young. At the same time I met their cousins the Chickadees as they visited and softly sang their lovely songs to Mrs. Titmice while she was confined to her house waiting for the young ones to arrive. A year later the three young ones return several times a day to eat and bathe.

I have been near nature most of my life, but this is the first time it became a part of my life. It could have resulted from unexpected health problems that kept me home bound, or from being in a new place without friends and family. Now I enjoy the friends God sends to my window. My new friends have taught me that I didn't have to travel the world to see and be with nature. It is everywhere. It is right outside my window.

About Mary Nida:

Mary Nida Smith was raised on a farm in Wisconsin. She lived in Oregon, Idaho, Washington along the Puget Sound) and in Arkansas, near lakes and forest. She has written for magazines, newspapers, and won awards for her photography. Smith is a member of the Ozarks Regional Arts Council, Free Verse Poetry Group and a volunteer at the Donald W. Regionals Library.

The Debussy Bird

By

Elisabeth Kinsey

The first time I heard a Canyon Wren on a hike in Boulder's Flatirons, I thought, *A-ha. That's where Claude Debussy was inspired to write Arabesque No. 1.* The Wren trills slowly, melodious and downward-sloping, just like Debussy's light fingers trailing down piano keys. The birdcall ends in three or four final rasps, as Arabesque No. 1's last bar continues in three gliding endnotes. I announced, "That's the Debussy bird!" to my hiking friend, Rob, who paused on the trail dripping in sweat, his face blank. I waved it off, "Never mind."

Don't get me wrong, I have friends who understand my ever-growing and cumulative awe of birds, but Rob wasn't one of them. Even as a child in California, I wondered from which birds the mocking bird stole its erratic yet heart-felt dupe-song. In my 40s, I'm still a bird novice. I still get tricked by the chickadee's many manifestations and I can't pin each Colorado bird's song to their body. Somehow, naming them lends respect yet widens their mystique.

I was pursuing a bachelor's degree in writing when I began a search for the 'Debussy bird' online. I'd get close, but then get sucked back into a heavy book- filled backpack world, birds an afterthought to homework. I was reminded again on Christmas break, while watching the Learning Channel program "Best Escapes," where a family hiked through Utah's Moab rock formations. I flipped through channels and heard an echo throughout the family's backpack trek. I raced to the TV and turned up the volume where the narrator's baritone resounded on walls and ceiling. The narrator's voice droned on about rock formations and in the background, there it was: Reet reet reet reet reet Da-deet, da-deet, da-deet, da-deet, da...da..da." I jumped up; book heaps falling to the floor, to declare to no one, "There he is again, damn-it!" Then, I touched the screen, like touching a mystery, and confronted him, "Who are you?"

After typing into Google every combination of birds and rocks, I found the website to ease any bird-lover's soul: All About Birds Guide. Then I finally named him: "Canyon Wren, Breeding Male, Resident from southern British Columbia southward through Pacific and Mountain states to Baja California and much of the Mexican interior, eastward to southwestern South Dakota and central Texas. Preferred habitats include cliffs, canyons, rocky outcrops, and boulder piles."

Bingo! I played the trill all afternoon in my office alternating it with a YouTube pianist playing Debussy's Arabesque No. 1. My dog rushed from room to room, looking for the intruder.

I continued to read about my Debussy bird. According to <Whatbird. com> its "tail is long and brown with thin black bars. Head has a flattened appearance; bill is long, slender, and slightly decurved."

In most ornithological reports, the Canyon Wren has an "open-cup, low-lying" nest and eats insects. This elusive bird only lives in dry regions, and usually makes its nests in "boulder piles" or high cliffs. He's not much to look at, with a dusty color with a grayish head. The distinguishing feature to me is his beak, or as experts call it "bill," that is skinny like a woodpecker's; I suppose it's to poke at all the critters in crevices. I'd actually spotted him on a hike and didn't know it, chalking it up to some kind of small woodpecker. I called my dad and left a message.

"Dad—I've found my Debussy bird. It's the Canyon Wren. Go to the website..."

Later, he called me back, questioning my excitement.

"Beth, you've always surprised me. You and Mary Oliver."

My dad introduced the nature-nut poetess to me in high school, so I knew he was just teasing. I stepped into a new realm of the bird-obsessors with the Canyon Wren, and I was happy to join them. Mary Oliver, Barry Lopez, Jonathan Evan Maslow, Terry Tempest Williams (to only name a few) all have leaned into their perspective worlds of birds, emerging with ornithological prose and worry for their habitat.

When Mary Oliver writes of owls, it's as if she's describing a torrid affair. Her breathlessness in the wake of these large creatures of the sky seems to transcribe onto the page in a fast scrawl. Of the great-horned owl she scribbles, "I'm struck, I'm taken, I'm conquered...I drop to the sand, I can't move; I am restless no more; I am replete, supine, finished, filled to the last edges with an immobilizing happiness. And is this not also terrible? Is this not also frightening?"

For some reason, picturing Oliver scribbling in fervor rather than crafting the poem over periods of months reveals the feeling I had upon hearing the Canyon Wren. With the same avid appetite, I called my next victim to explain the inspiration for Debussy's Arabesque No.1.

My fellow bird friend, Melanie, knowing well how I give in to week-long obsessions, joined my bird-hunt.

"I wonder if Claude Debussy was hiking and wrote it?" I asked her since her husband studied music.

"No idea," she said, which sent us to look up Eastern France and Debussy's birthplace.

There were no connections with the Canyon Wren or Saint-Germain-en-Laye, Yvelines, France. Nothing came up with Debussy and the Canyon Wren combination, either. We retreated into the Birding websites; Melanie shouted out random birds she'd studied in her freshman nature course, and played the Canyon Wren over and over to hear the trill. Even though we didn't get close to any connections between the Canyon Wren and Arabesque No. 1, we discovered that the French wren is a chunkier version of its rock-hiding brother and its call is higher and less melodic. Debussy would have had to hike amongst rocks or cliffs somewhere in United States, - a far cry from his own habitat - to have been inspired by the Canyon Wren.

As I came up with no impetus for Debussy's Arabesque No. 1 being inspirationally derived from the Canyon Wren, I went back to Boulder's Chautauqua hiking trails with the goal of hearing the Canyon Wren's heart-breaking trill once again. The shallow bit of the trail without rocks ends abruptly at a tree line. My fellow hikers weren't as game to enter Shadow Canyon, which is purely vertical for at least three hours. I know because I had once made it to the top. Everyone abandoned me and I went a little farther, almost reaching a boulder the size of my body. After two more turns into pine trees, the forest floor rising up with its pine and damp, I still hadn't heard the familiar trill. I looked at the next rock outcropping a few feet in the distance and waited. Not a sound. My wren would not appear on cue.

To satisfy my yen for melody, I looked up a list of Northern Colorado birds. I went to each bird, copied and pasted it into the All About Birding website, hoping to identify any familiar voices I'd heard in my backyard. A few revealed themselves. My cat hates the Northern Flickers with their humorous "wucka wuckas." She'll sit at the lawn's edge and sniff at them, while my dog stands at the screen, watching the Wood Doves nestled on the ledge as they settle into the day on my front porch.

Ornithologists translate bird calls into word sounds to communicate how birds sound. Next to an illustration of the Canyon Wren's gray-blue body it reads "peter;peter;peter, peto,peto,peto." It's a happy, see-saw kind of twitter. I don't pretend to be an ornithologist at all, only an enthusiast. It's one of those hobbies creeping into life and the discovery of other bird-calls was anti-climatic to my Canyon Wren's trill connection.

The translation for the Canyon Wren's call on my bird website is "Peup, peup, peup tew tew tew tew tew mew", "jeet." The last comma and "jeet" don't at all resemble its dramatic last lines. I listen to its call almost as compulsively as people who make the same mistake repeatedly. Looking for other such compulsive Wren followers, I came upon a fellow Canyon Wren enthusiast, Bob Ribokas. He discounts it slightly when he describes its call as "a strong series of whistles that continuously descends in pitch from the start to the end of the call." Whistles? I disagree. But then I'm with Ribokas as he claims, "Many a trip into the inner-depths of the Canyon has been brightened by the companionship of the Canyon Wren...When you hear one give its call in a narrow, enclosed area and it echoes [sic] off of the high cliffs that are all around you, it is much more unforgettable. I will never forget the Canyon Wren."

Luis Felipe Baptista, a Zoologist and Ornithologist, made bird-song his life-long study. In an article about bird-song, he conjectures that birds are "vocalists and instrumentalists" and connects the European Starling as having inspired Mozart. I can go on legitimizing my fling with ornithology, but I know I'm missing the goods: Debussy's inspiration.

As I listen to the Canyon Wren's call, I feel certain that somewhere in Debussy's journals, there must be at least one line where he is flattened by its beauty, where his heart leaps and he is "filled to the last edges with an immobilizing happiness." I hope a musicologist takes on the challenge to find the link between Claude Debussy and the Canyon Wren. Maybe a distant Debussy cousin who remembers a nature walk among hanging rocks will put the two together? Perhaps he has a memory where they were suddenly filled with amazing birdsong and the cousin notes Debussy scribbling hard in his journal. Until then, I'm forever changed by the Canyon Wren's trill and influence over my life. I have entered into the realm of air and sky, the tiny beats of our lives above us, emitting joy in unique conversation.

"So quickly, without a moment's warning, does the miraculous swerve and point to us, demanding that we be its willing servant." -Mary Oliver, *Blue Pastures*

About Elisabeth:

Elisabeth Kinsey was born in northern California and raised amongst her Italian and Jewish families. Her parents converted to Mormonism, which is the basis of her memoir: The Holy Ghost Goes to Bed at Midnight: Half a Mormon Life. She has a BA in Writing at Metropolitan State University of Denver and her MA in Creative Writing at Regis University. She teaches writing and composition at Regis University. Her published works appear in Greenwoman Magazine, Ask Me About My Divorce, Seal Press, Wazee Journal, The Rambler and Emergency Press, among other journals.

Bleeding Heart

By

Nikki Rosen

Near the end of last summer, I took my twelve year old daughter, Sarah, to a local nursery. Her eyes lit up when she saw the Bleeding Heart plant. She begged me to buy it for her.

"I don't know," I told her. I looked at the tag. It had been marked down more than fifty percent from its original price. I looked at Sarah and shook my head. "It costs ten dollars, still a bit too pricey."

"I really want it," Sarah begged.

"You would need to be responsible," I said.

"I promise I will." Her big, brown eyes pleaded with me. "I want it, Ma. I already have a name picked out for her."

"A name?"

"I'm going to call her Sophie."

My heart melted. Reluctantly, I dug into my purse.

True to her word, my daughter showered the plant with love, pride and undivided attention. At the first snowfall, Sarah wanted to run outside and cover Sophie with a blanket, but I pulled her close, told her she was a great little mom and that Sophie would be fine.

In April, I needed to move some things around in the garden. Without thinking, I plopped a large basket near the back gate. A few weeks later, my daughter looked out the window to see if Sophie had returned. She hadn't. And then I heard an anguished cry. "Maaaaa!"

The two of us ran outside. I lifted the basket. There was Sophie -

squished into the ground.

"You killed her!"

"Don't panic. Maybe she'll come back."

My daughter raised her eyebrows at me, but for the next few days while she watered, I prayed. Every day Sarah ran outside and checked on Sophie. She scraped away all the debris left from the winter and gently padded the soil around the stem. I felt a twinge of guilt when I heard her whisper to the little plant, "Please come back."

To our amazement, Sophie did revive. This time she came back stronger and taller and fuller than before. Sarah whooped and hollered. Her hard work and love had paid off.

The experience with Sophie reminded me of something I've witnessed time and time again. I work in the field of social work and have had the privilege to be on the journey with many women who have experienced unthinkable traumas, losses and pain. Similar to Sophie, their resilience to survive pushes them against the hardness of life and they too come back stronger and with greater confidence.

Nature has always been where I've found inspiration and teachable lessons. A few years back, I visited my sister in Israel. She took me to the top of a rocky mountain. Nothing was there except rock, stones and gravel. I remember standing there and feeling like I could touch the sky. The two of us sat for a long time remembering the terrible beatings, abuse and isolation we both experienced at the hands of our parents.

I'm not sure why we hadn't noticed them before, but there a few feet from us, two flowers were growing in the rocks. We were stunned. How could those two flowers grow in the middle of all that hardness? How could they survive and grow? Somehow they had managed to survive without adequate soil or proper care. I looked at my sister. "We survived."

"But how did we survive?"

I looked up at the sky. I remember when my mother was dying. We lived in a tight Jewish community. I came home from school and found a Catholic nun sitting with our mother. I think that woman prayed for us. And I think God heard.

Thinking about those two flowers, I wonder if He put them there to show us, even in the hard places, He's there helping us to grow, helping us to be strong, keeping us safe.

Nature has a pull, a tug that draws me. I spend considerable time in the hills near our home, hiking the wooded trails. It's where I feel free and yet connected. Wandering the mountains and breathing in the smells, sounds and sights has been the greatest way of healing my life. I always return home feeling renewed and full of hope.

About Nikki:

Nikki Rosen has authored two books, In the Eye of Deception: A True Story *– winner of The Word Guild Award and* Dancing Softly, *shortlisted for The Word Guild Award. She's been published in various anthologies and magazines. She can be reached at www. write2empower.webs.com*

River Knots

By

Rose McMackin

It was a sticky, hot summer day and I was killing time. We were sitting in his truck in a parking lot in California. Like me, he'd been living on the road for months now. There was a toothbrush in the cup holder.

"Look at this," he said.

He picked up a piece of wood from the dashboard and handed it to me. It looked like a knuckle the size of a human heart. He selected it from a variety of geological and botanical specimens that he had lined up along the curved base of his windshield.

"This is a river knot," he told me.

As kayakers, we know that logs in rivers function like colanders. These old bones block the movement of solid things, while water appears simply to accept what is and goes around the blockage. We also know that, over a long enough time, water will cut through anything. Eventually, inevitably, water wins. It wears wood away to pulp, pulling pieces away, fiber by fiber.

Somehow though, these chunks remain. At the joint where a branch emerges from a tree, the wood is cross-grained and stronger. The weaker wood that encompasses them is slowly pulled away. The knots are beaten out by years of flow and washed downstream. They spin in eddies until they're made polished and spherical. They float in eddies for years, until someone - like you or me - picks them up. It takes someone who recognizes them for the rare chunks of organic matter that they are; fibrous survivors of years of river wear.

He explained all this to me with an almost distressing intensity. It impresses me sometimes ("Never cheat a rapid that you've run before"), and sometimes it unsettles me, how he can find a way to snarl out even the most innocuous sentiments.

This afternoon in his truck was the last of just a few days that I had spent with him. Water drew him east, other rivers called me north. Or more specifically, I flitted north to kayak the temperate rain forests of Southern Washington.

I found whitewater— at least partially— because I wanted to fall in love with an outdoors boy. I say partially because I did choose kayaking. I gravitated towards the free fall of whitewater when I could have been a climber or mountain biker or backpacker; when the gender odds would have fallen equally in my favor no matter which outdoor community I ended up in. Oh, those absurd gender ratios. That should've been my first clue about what kind of person it takes.

This is a strange life I've chosen, a life that requires absolute single-mindedness. You must possess a certain grandiose faith in your own infallibility to gain entry to this world. Kayaking has cost me dearly at times, in wildly divergent ways. I have driven cross-country for 52-hours straight on Taco Bell takeout and no sleep. I have frozen my fingers past the point of pain and smashed my face on rocks. I have been to funerals. It's the kind of thing that I post to my blog and then pray my parents don't read. And of course, getting good at kayaking meant demoting other interests I had once loved, like photography and traveling in Europe. I've sacrificed all this because I can't imagine my life without the river.

But the struggle is undermined, not only by love of wildness, but by the undeniable excitement of being a woman in this rugged world.

And so, in that way, I was naive about obsession, and surprised when my first river boyfriend left me for the Snake River with the parting words "I want to follow my dreams and I want you to follow yours." And I was surprised again when the next one— he was only a boater to fill the off-season around skiing— left me for Japanese white powder.

From the moment I realized that no transient river boy was going to love me more than he already loved the river, I wanted to live that life: self-contained, unconcerned with human relationships. I wanted to strike out on a transcontinental whitewater, self-discovery adventure of Jack Kerouac proportions, without even a whiff of a romantic subplot. Maybe it's because I envy these men with their dissociation, or maybe I just like to be contrary. I have read that the female brain is more preoccupied with building and maintaining relationships than the male brain— that some professor at the University of Texas concluded that men derive their self-confidence from the ability to maintain independence, while women are confident based on their ability to build and maintain intimacy. But I hate the thought that a neurological fundamental has set me up for a preexisting image of my outdoor experience, or that a biological imperative has me poised as supporting someone else's character.

So I will, for a moment, make an argument for nurture over nature. Independence is a muscle that I am learning to develop as systematically as my laterals and triceps. Once upon a time, I thought that I wanted to find a boy who wouldn't leave me for fresh snow melt. There was a moment when I would've followed that first boy to the Snake River, but in the end, it was just that: a moment. Because now it seems that when I find those boys, I end up leaving them for rivers of my own choosing.

I am getting older now and years of water have beaten me out to be something different than I was. My heart has been hardened in its own way— it's not quite as hard as wood, but it's tough— by these rough, rowdy characters who move through and around me. They knock against me, and pull pieces away with me in their comings and goings. I have learned to let things affect me; shape me, without containing me. Like their unsolicited chunks of advice - delivered with such inappropriate ferocity, making them so unforgettable.

Because I knew that if I left on a whim to run the White Salmon, he might be gone before I was back, and that it would make that day in the truck an unanticipated, anticlimactic ending. That evening, when he dropped me off, neither one of us had thought to linger on the word "goodbye," both assuming it was really more of a "see you later." And of course, I always want to say a real goodbye when it's called for, but I wanted that river more. Like I said, in the end, water always wins.

About Rose:

Rose McMackin is a 23-year-old California native. A fondness for the romantics led her to work as a wilderness guide and the sport of whitewater kayaking, both of which she now pursues with a zeal that would make Thoreau proud. She chronicles a life of adventure and commitment-phobia at www.rosemcmackin.com.

Wild Strawberries

By

Nancy Cook

This was a perfect garden. Harmonious, a symphony of color: pink peonies and purple primrose, oxlip gold, bluebells hung from fiddle bows, and campanula cupped to capture echoes wind-chimed from the patio. It is a fine-tuned orchestration, with every species staged to bloom on cue- magnolia, phlox, and iris; yarrow, catnip, sage, verbena, lilies, roses, beebalm, daisies, roses, and asters. A sunny tract pampers round-faced rampion, her feathery curls a la fascinators bound for ascot or the henley regatta. Flirty cowslip nods and waves, bestirring willowy lavender. Red-capped pokers, erect and prim as ushers, cinch corners, their disciplined stature lending an air of dignity to the scene. On the ground, gracing the fresh soil, were a few fallen petals, just enough to assure environmental veritas. Even the butterflies seemed ideally placed.

Our sandals slid on bleached stones like fingertips on ivories. We strolled at leisure, but at a pace that seemed somehow predetermined. A table at the far end is set for tea. Champagne awaited in fluted glasses: too petite for snobbishness, they tinkle as they touch. Bubbles floated in atmospheric grace toward clouds - not clouds, really, just slight erasure marks on the sky. And in a Waterford bowl, strawberries as pink as blushing cheeks, dipped in Swiss chocolate, coolly repose on beds of ice.

Unencumbered by the combustible shells of shoulds and oughts threatening daily to explode in the chaos of life, I succumbed to the respite offered by this holiday outing with friends and garden enthusiasts. The school term had just ended, and I was still recovering and reeling from it all. The most recent conference with Mary's two teachers and the academic counselor started, as such meetings always do, with assurances of how much everyone loves Mary. She is so creative, so bright, so enthusiastic, so eager to contribute. Yes, she is always respectful, and no, she is never disruptive. But we can't understand why Mary refuses to do homework, and why she will not follow directions and complete assignments.

The educators ran through the usual list of possible diagnoses, none of which could be made to fit. I offered up the latest professional opinion, executive dysfunction, suggested by the twelfth or eighteenth or thirtieth expert who'd been consulted. It was promptly rejected by the group. According to one, "That's what people say when they can't think of any other excuse." I countered with, "Don't you think, if she could control this, Mary would?" and other similar rationales. What swiftly followed were hints of parenting failure, and the insistence that there must be consequences for nonconformance.

It was after this conference that twelve-year-old Mary was given a choice: to complete every assignment on time, or be confined in a windowless room adjacent to the headmistress's office - a room no larger than a broom closet - until the work was done. Deprived of social intercourse, not to mention light and fresh air, Mary began to wilt. One morning before breakfast I found her still in her bed, knotted into a fetal position. So, after a week of the school's remedy, during which, no surprise to me, not a single homework assignment was completed, I freed my daughter from the environment intended to foster learning. For the final month of the term, Mary was subjected only to my attempts at home-schooling cramped between other domestic obligations and the nagging demands of my work.

Mary went off to an overnight camp, where she could thrive in sunshine and summer breezes and rain, charm the camp counselors, make best friends with a half dozen newly-blossoming adolescents, and explore the natural limits of the world.

This was my chance, too, to find renewal in the outdoors.

At the perfect garden our group of ladies spread a blanket on the close-shorn grass, and arranged ourselves for some chitchat. It's all in the planning, the hostess says, in polite reply to murmurings of envious admiration. Of course, we all know it isn't so; even the rankest amateur comprehends the truth about a garden's mollycoddling, the hours pulling stubborn weeds; pruning eager, greedy branches; plucking yellowed leaves; negotiating space for stragglers; and healing blights and sweat and tears.

"Flowers are like children", someone observed.

Yes, and rules require enforcement, lessons must be minded, scales must be practiced, and homework must be completed.

Our hostess, soft-spoken and as gracious as she appeared, must once have been an iron-willed nanny or the strictest sort of parent; she had to be. Only a person with staff sergeant sensibilities could command such a high level of obedience from her plants. I dropped my chin in an involuntarily acknowledgement of my shame. Maybe I really was to blame for Mary's school problems.

Eyes lowered now, I noticed something. Shaded by the steps that lead up to the gate, cushioned by leafy greens as dense as wooly carpet patches, I spied vagabonds: uninvited guests who detected opportunity in the concrete fold where a sharply angled footpath and stone steps diverge, creating hidden cracks. Occupying those spaces were tiny fruits, redder than a parrot's wing, oblivious to rules and reason, and undeniable: Wild strawberries.

Glancing up, I saw the hostess eyeing me. I saw her slight smile, a smile that recalled another, from a photograph in the entryway through which we passed en route to the gardens. The photo was of a granddaughter perhaps, or a godchild or a niece, six or eight years old, caught mid-jump on a trampoline, lost in the extravagance of flight. In this quiet moment of recollection, I understood that I had found an ally in a master landscaper who, with all her skill in cultivating the finest flowers and staging their emergence, shared my own secret conviction about growing things. I understood. The wild berries were for the granddaughter or godchild or niece, for all the restless children, giddy in discovery. And in that perfect garden, I took joy not just from the exquisite flora and their surroundings, but from those red berries, infantine and fragile as a robin's eggs, that have no need to be civilized by chocolate dip, however velvety or rich.

About Nancy:

Nancy Cook is a writer, teacher, community lawyer, and parent living in the northern U.S. Her work has appeared in numerous publications in the U.S., Australia, and the U.K. She runs the "Witness Project," a series of community workshops for populations underserved by the justice system. This past summer, she also ran "justice writing" workshops in England and Wales.

Featuring: Lynx Vilden

Introduction by Carol Clouse

My favorite quote from Lynx Vilden's Living Wild website refers to the message she wishes to emblazon upon her students. She speaks of them *"experiencing the inter-dependency necessary in community living"* and of nurturing in them *"an appreciation for the Earth as a living organism."* Nature is all encompassing, and human beings oft seem to forget that we are all an intertwined part of a connected living cosmos.

In 2001 Lynx started her own school, *Living Wild,* with the intention of leading participants through a series of skills classes in which they create a set of prehistoric gear including tools, containers, weapons, clothing and bedding, entirely from the elements of stone, bone, wood and animal skins. For a month after these preparations, students and teacher wander the wilderness of the mountains, hunting, gathering, and connecting with nature. Her school is based out of Washington, and classes are held throughout Washington, Montana, and Oregon.

It was after Lynx had spent eight years as a vegetarian that she tells me she killed her first chicken. At the age of 24, she explains that this was also the advent of her delving deep into the realm of primitive technology that she has been practicing and teaching ever since. She shares with me that "these forays into the wilds have led me into previously unimaginable connections with the mineral, plant and animal kingdoms as well as new insights into the development of community within my own species and our relationship with the living Earth."

Lynx is truly an inspiration to her students and, as every teacher knows, when we teach, we continue to learn. As Lynx declares on her website, "This school is not our job; it's our way of life." In reading the following pages, we all become one of Lynx's students. We all get a taste of the simple joy of – *Living Wild.*

www.lynxvilden.com

Colors of a Woman

By

Lynx Vilden

I am a woman.

I lie in long grass, yellowed by the passage of summer. It is the same color as my hair. Clouds drift solemnly from the West, blue sky, dappled with white. .

Close by, a spotted horse, black on white, tears at the yellowing grass.

Beside me is a yellow bow. I wear a red dress. I am waiting for the deer.

I haven't yet said my prayer or made any offering. These things are important to me, what shall I give?

The wind. It rises and falls. I hear it coming in the tops of the green pines and then it is upon me in the grass, passing by and another gust builds in its wake.

The yellow bow is unstrung, hanging on a branch together with a quiver full of arrows. The bow tells a story. For me, the story starts in a Montana woodshed where a pile of Osage-orange staves have been curing for several years; I traded my friend for one that I picked out myself. Bright yellow curls of wood fell to the ground steadily as I shaped it. The stave became a bow. This bow has taken life but it has not taken a deer.

With my knife I cut a swatch of my yellow hair, and with a piece of fading yellow grass tie it onto a branch in the tree that I lie beneath. My prayer is for a clean, peaceful kill.

I have shot a few deer, three to be exact, but with a rifle. It's very different, the shocking violence of the explosion. I clearly remember all three of them. I could go to the exact same spot again and tell you how they died.

My first prayer was *Teach me everything I need to know about taking life.* It was a hard lesson.

That frosty November morning, my feet crunching as silently as feet crunching can be. The first deer and the peace shattering bullet that missed. Later, the two does that diagonally cut down the slope toward the creek, unaware of my presence. The raised rifle, the long shot considered and the slow squeeze of the trigger.

Karma is the name of the spotted horse that I rode here today. She's a three year old Appaloosa. I kind of dreamed her into my life. Before I ever met her I envisioned her steaming warm breath on my cheek. I knew she was coming. "Bring me a spotted horse with no saddle....." There was this book I read about a girl called Pippi Longstocking. She was the strongest girl in the world and she had a spotted horse. I always wanted to be like Pippi when I was a kid. Guess I still do.

Image provided by Lynx Vilden

So I went to look at a herd of Appaloosas. She wasn't the prettiest of them all, this gangly, un-broken teenager but she came up to me. She liked me. I wanted to check her out, away from the others and see her move, get a feel for who she was. The only way to take her that day was through a barn that had about thirty huge, barking dogs penned up on both sides of the walkway. She had never walked through there before or been away from the herd. I whispered in her ear "If you are my spotted horse, will you follow me through this?" It was a big deal. It was intense for me too. We walked through the gauntlet, together, she trusting me. When we came out the other side I had tears running down my face, she chose me. "Let's go home." I picked her up the next day. That was three months ago.

I am a daughter.

All of us women are, whether or not we know or love those that gave us our bodies. I will still be a daughter when both my parents are gone from this world, held in the divine embrace of the Earth.

I was born in a city far across the ocean.

Blue. The ocean reflecting the sky, the same color as my eyes.

My mother was a textile artist. She met my father on a boat going to England with a friend. I have seen photos of that journey, that first meeting, the young women and the young men, smiling and laughing. I can easily imagine the smell of the salty air, the cry of gulls, and the spray of the dark North Sea. There is excitement in their faces. I too have traveled that same route many times.

When I was a young child I learned to swim in a lake surrounded by a forest in Sweden. The lake was named after the smallest coin, we would call it 'dime lake' I suppose. It was icy cold but I didn't care. I would jump off the wooden dock, over and over and paddle around until my lips were blue and I couldn't stop shivering. That's hypothermia, I know that now. All I knew then was how much fun I was having and the promise of a big fluffy towel and a warm lap made the teeth chattering cold really okay.

I remember too a night in a small wooden cabin near that lake. I woke up in the silence, deep in the moonless forest, opening my eyes to find that not the tiniest amount of light was available to give me any shape or form in that consuming darkness. It's rare for us sighted beings to experience that total blackness. I was frightened back then. I finally found comfort in the faint points of luminosity shed by the numbers on my wrist watch. I was still alive.

I had a dream recently. I was going down in a plane. The crash was imminent. I knew I was going to die. This feeling of peace washed over me and I closed my eyes and started saying "I love you, I love you, I love you……" Then the impact, so this was death finally? My words however, continued but they had changed slightly, "I am love, I am love, I am love."

I opened my eyes to find that I was not dead but awake.

Here now, the sky with its solemn clouds has faded. I lay down in the grass, wriggling into my sleeping bag, throwing my coat over my feet. I know the dew will soak me. My clothes are piled under my head for a pillow.

A bright star is visible, a planet probably. Suddenly, as if by consensus, the familiar patterns leap simultaneously into the sky. The Big Dipper, pointing North, no surprises, I am familiar, at home in this land. Tonight there is a moon, waxing in its third quarter. The hills glow across the river, illuminated. The blue sky turned to black, yellow grass to grey.

I hear the deer all around me, grazing in the moonlight.

I am a mother.

Not every woman shares the story of carrying child within her womb or expelling a slippery body in a gush of blood.

Blood. Red. Red is the color of my dress.

Yes, I am and have a daughter. Her hair and eyes are the same color as mine but that is another story. My dress is red.

The crisp November air shattered as the doe fell and started crawling desperately on her front two legs, paralyzed in the rear. I shot again, shaking, my shot missed. I shot a third time and missed again.

I realized at this point that I had only one more bullet in my rifle, had to get closer. I ran down the bank and across the creek, now I could see the panic in her eyes. I made careful aim at her head, pulled...click. Nothing, I had miss-counted, I was out of bullets.

Shaking and crying I thought about my prayer "everything I need to know about taking life...." I would have to kill her with my knife?

Just then as this reality started to grimly sink in I heard the sound of an angel coming to my rescue. The angel was driving a full-size pick-up as angels tend to do on Montana back roads. I ran back up the hill and waved it to a stop, the window rolled down and a blue haired, kindly looking grandma sort gazed at me. I blurted out my story.... *shot and wounded a deer and run out of bullets,* I didn't really know what to expect.

"What caliber?" she drawled.

"30/30" I answered.

Incredulous. I watched her open a giant container full of bullets, rummage around and hand me one, then drive away without another word. The bullet does its job, I am spared. Blood stains the snow together with my tears.

The morning air is still, a faint brightness on the Eastern horizon. The dew in little pearls all covering the flattened grass around me. Some deer stamp and snort nearby as they catch my scent or hear me rustling as I turn over. My bow is still unstrung beside me. I dream some more, the comfort of the ground beneath me, the cozy warmth of my bed.

Now it is light. Pale, rosy red clouds grace the sky. I sit up and look around. A doe is looking straight at me. I duck back down below the tall grass, reach for the yellow bow and string it with difficulty, staying as low as possible. Pulling an arrow from the quiver and slinging the rest over my shoulder I crouch-crawl to the cover of the pines. She doesn't stop looking at me. Slowly the white flag tail goes up. She snorts and starts the cautious, deliberate pacing away from perceived threat. No overt panic or flight but she is not going to stick around.

I walk the tree line on the edge of the clearing. Feet soaking wet. I clear the meadow and meander up a familiar trail making a big arc. I see half a dozen more deer, one even in range, but they are all hip to me and bound away before I have a chance to string an arrow.

Why do I do this? I am not a hunter and yet I hunt. I do not want to kill the deer. I want to BE the deer. I am a mother, I have birthed. It is not my instinct to kill. I believe that men were made for that task. We bring life into the world. They take it in order to sustain us all. Yet, I eat and I enjoy eating meat, I want to take responsibility for this exchange of life and death, and so I walk this autumn morning, bow in hand, hunting.

I am a goddess.

Co-creator of my destiny. I wrote a song about that once, calling it "When I am an old woman." I heard this name, Shuwah-Awah, in a dream. Maybe I will become her someday. All the verses in the song are filled with the things that I want to do in my life. I wrote them down so they could start being arranged in the Universe. That's the way to do it you know, just think it up, speak it out, write it down and watch it unfold.

When I am an old woman I'll be friends with the trees,
Climb high in their branches of needles and leaves,
And together so softly, Shuwah-Awah,
They will tell me their tales of their power.

I look at the green firs and pines around me, conifers...evergreen. Green is my favorite color.

After I killed that first doe, I skinned and gutted her there in the snow. I spent that entire winter using every single scrap of her body, her flesh and organs fed my family, her bones became tools, beads, a flute, her hooves a rattle and her skin part of this red dress that I am wearing.

The stories are thick and numerous. I can still see the yellow butterfly that landed on a red and yellow sandstone cobble in a trickling creek in the painted Arizona desert. I took that sandstone and used it to shape those bones that I use still. That rattle continues its story, passed on to coastal natives who gifted my people with salmon. All of life is imbued with stories if we care to remember and repeat them.

I hear a rustle behind me. I turn and a deer, startled, bounds past me, barely twenty yards away, a muley doe. She stops and I sink into the grass nocking an arrow. I whisper almost inaudibly.

"Are you offering yourself to me? Come closer."

She walks in tight circles, stiff-legged, curious, on high alert. She moves a little closer, sniffing the air. The wind is in my favor....nineteen, eighteen yards, still out of range for my wooden bow.

"Will you give yourself to me?"

Gradually I crawl toward her. I feel utterly feline, limbs smoothly, stealthily inching closer, mind, single-focused, absolutely present. She backs off, high stepping, stiff, tight little circles. Slowly I rise to my knees. I've gained ten yards and lost as many. A pine tree shields me from her view and I take a few quicker steps.

"Are you?"

She is not. She bounds, four legs in the air. She is not giving herself to me. Not now, not today. All the while I was wondering......*Would I take you even if you offered?* I still don't know the answer.

When I am an old woman I shall run with the deer,
I'll talk with the eagle, the fish and the bear, A
nd the animals call me Shuwah-Awah,
And the grasshoppers sing, Shuwah-Awah.

I look around me at all the colors; yellow, blue, red, green and all the shades and hues and textures. What a marvelous and mysterious creation.

Image provided by Lynx Vilden

145

In the Woods

By

Nalani Askov

It was the summer after my life fell apart and there I was, camped at the Elkhart Park trailhead in the northern part of the Wind River Range, watching hail the size of quarters pelt my Volkswagen camper van so hard I was sure the windows were going to shatter. It was the evening before an overnight shakedown hike to Miller Lake that was supposed to help me acclimate to the atmosphere at 10,000 feet. I had driven to Wyoming from Seattle as part of a three month sabbatical from my law practice. My own exacting nature combined with years of long hours, constant stress, anxiety, and the work of investigating the depths of the most appalling employee behaviors, had finally broken me. I was depressed and floundering. When my law partnership dissolved as a result, I was freed to take significant time off from work for the first time since I left home at age 17. I was getting healthier but still needed time away to fully recover and decide what was next in my life.

The following morning, the skies had cleared and my windshield mercifully remained unbroken from the hail. I balanced my camera on the van and took a cheesy picture of myself loaded up with gear before heading out for the four- mile hike to Miller Lake. I slipped a whistle lanyard over my head, knowing it would stay there until I returned. It had long been my dream to hike in the Winds and next week, I was planning to do a weeklong 35 mile round trip to Titcomb Basin. The hike to Miller Lake would be a small test of my stamina, my new ultralight gear, and most importantly, the strength of my mental state.

The wide shady trail through the forest turned into a gradual uphill tread before a steep switchback down to the lake. I arrived at the lake by mid-day, earlier and more tired from the altitude than I expected. Branching off from the main trail around the south side of the small lake, I found a well-trodden spur that led straight up the hillside. I hiked about 100 yards uphill, my heart pounding from the effort in the thin air. At the top, I discovered a large flat campsite on a bench with a panoramic view of the lake and the mountains beyond. Many people had obviously camped at this site before, as evidenced by a giant stone fire pit that had been added to over time and now looked like something that belonged in a suburban backyard instead of a wilderness area.

I pitched my tent with the back up against a large boulder and then scouted around before finally finding another area 100 yards away with a tree big enough to hang my food and cooking gear. I tossed my bear bag over a tree limb, hauled up one food and cooking sack with the parachute cord, and in counter-weight style, tied off and pushed the second bag up with my outstretched hiking pole.

I walked back to camp, grabbed the four piece fly rod I had strapped to my pack, popped the tiny fly box filled with barbless flies I used for backpacking into my shirt pocket, and pinned a pair of nail clippers on a zinger onto my shirt. I removed the large canister of bear spray from my pack strap and clipped it to my belt. I headed down to the lake to try my luck at fishing from some of the large boulders along the shore. After catching and releasing a few small brightly colored brook trout, I washed my hands in the lake, scrubbing them with sand and grit to get rid of the fish smell before heading back to camp.

Dinner that night was a steel pint cup full of instant hot curried couscous, cashews and dried cranberries mixed with some freeze-dried veggies. Dessert was M&M's sifted from my bag of trail mix. Quick, neat and not too smelly. That night after dinner, I carefully changed out of my "cooking" clothes and stashed them in my pack about 50 yards away. I foraged around the hillside and after about an hour had finally gathered a large pile of wood. As it grew dark, I built a big fire in the stone fire pit and sat on a nearby log listening to the night sounds, reading my map and thinking about the Titcomb Basin trip.

At first, the warmth and light of the fire, the bright stars and cool evening were a pleasant comfort. But soon the darkness loomed around me. My heart jumped a little at every rustle. I turned, shining my headlamp toward the sounds and shadows that danced menacingly in the trees and bushes around camp. I fingered the large canister of bear spray by my side, making sure it was in the right position for immediate use. After a while - even with the large fire - the plummeting night temperatures that come at 10,000 feet forced me into my down sleeping bag. Before getting into my tent, I stoked the fire extra high. I figured bears wouldn't come near a fire. I carefully tucked my bear spray canister exactly at hand's reach next to me in my tent so I could find it in the dark. I kept the rain fly open so I could see the fire outside.

As I lay in my tent, I was acutely aware of how alone and vulnerable I was. My anxiety was on high alert and morbid, irrational fears plagued my mind. I had hiked alone many times but tonight my mind was obsessed with bears. All night, I tried to sleep but started at the slightest sound, certain that it was a bear. Surely I wouldn't make it through the night – a small depressed part of me half hoping that were true. I imagined what I would do if a bear came into camp; what I would do if it attacked; what if my bear canister didn't work; what its fur would feel and smell like; how I would try to fight off the bear if attacked at night in my tent. My depressed mind was in 'fight or flight' overdrive.

Sometime in the early morning hours, the fatigue, the exhaustion of constant adrenaline, and the fog of altitude, finally switched off my brain. I dozed off and awoke to a bright blue sky, the sun already at mid-morning. The fire was still smoldering. At that moment, I was glad to be alive. Happy no bear had visited me in the night. Pleased that my careful planning – washing my hands, carefully hanging my food, eating away from camp, changing my clothes, building a big fire – had kept harm at bay.

I started to walk down the small trail from my camp to the lake to filter some water for my morning coffee and there, in the mud, were the large clear imprints of a bear's paws where none had been the day before. I froze, took the safety off my bear spray canister and scanned the bushes for movement. If there was still a bear around, I didn't see or hear it. I carefully made my way down to the lake to fetch some water.

My plan had been to spend two nights at the lake to get used to the altitude but now there was at least one bear around. I sat on a big flat rock at my cooking spot, eating a couple of granola bars and boiling water on my 'Pocket Rocket' to make coffee. I looked at the woods around me, the blue sky, and the view down to the small rock rimmed lake. It was quiet, I was alone, it was beautiful – the perfect place and moment – except for the bears. My fearful obsession was threatening this trip and the one I had planned to Titcomb Basin.

I thought about all those precautions I had taken to ensure safety and maintain control. It was how I had always lived my life – planning for the worst, carefully gauging every risk, always having a back up plan – hazards of my profession and especially of my temperament, a consequence of a childhood filled with too much fearful watching and waiting. How could I have failed so miserably – a bear's tracks so close to my camp? I felt the frustration of a fundamental fact: bears would always be in the woods, uncontrollable and dangerous.

And then, just as quickly and deeply as I felt my failure, I suddenly knew that I could take as many precautions as I wanted; in fact, I could be perfect and it might not be good enough. If I wanted to be out here, to enjoy this wild land that I loved, I had to accept, embrace even, the fact that bears were always in the woods. In that moment, I realized it was also that way in life – there was always going to be danger – real and imagined, past and present – to be faced every day. That despite all our precautions, each of us eventually will die. Something uncontrollable will come to claim us.

"The bear is always in the woods" became my mantra that day – my commitment to live in spite of fear. That phrase became my promise to myself to live my life and the acknowledgement of its truth, a reconciliation of sorts between my dreams for the future and the traumatic unchangeable history of my childhood.

I spent the rest of that day dismantling the huge stone fire pit so many others had built. I carted water from the lake to wet the smoldering ashes from my own fire the night before. If I couldn't carry a rock away, I rolled it. After all the rocks were scattered, I scooped up and sprinkled the mounds of cold charred wood and ash into the thick bushes. Finally, I covered the scarred area with fresh earth and pine needles until it was restored; indistinguishable from the wilderness around it. Exhausted and filthy with soot, I washed up, changed clothes and had dinner.

That night, I built a very small fire on the bare earth in front of my tent, feeling its warmth burning close to me. Lying in my sleeping bag, I watched the fire burn out into darkness, which was much closer now, and I slept soundly knowing I was where I wanted to be and that yes, the bear would always be in the woods.

About Nalani:

Nalani Askov is an attorney and non-profit consultant in Seattle. Nalani was formerly the Executive Director of Washington Wild and the Jackson Hole Wildlife Foundation. She earned a BA in English at the University of Washington and a JD from the University of Washington School Of Law.

The Enchanted Earth

Linda Littlefield Grenfell

Where's Linda?" Sooner or later someone would notice that I was missing. Maybe it was time for dinner, or a bath, or bed. As the youngest it was easy to escape, everyone too busy to notice me. So I wandered.

Our acre of land had trees with long hanging branches where I could play with my dolls or just lie on the fragrant ground. The cemetery right beside my house was overgrown and magical, and I could scramble through the weeds and wonder at the people buried there. It was easy to get away.

As I got a little older 'The Enchanted Forest' beckoned; a field rich in wild strawberries, juniper, sweet fern, clover and especially pine trees. They were short and scrubby, easy to climb, enchanting and enticing. The field sloped down to the creek. We used the old English pronunciation 'crick', and I envied my mother who told stories of fishing, swimming, and boating on the 'crick'. By the time I arrived it was an open cesspool; raw sewage poured into it from the housing projects.

But the trees were inviting, cool and embracing. I could climb and hide and imagine. I pretended I was a Native American, following tracks, tasting berries, pretending to hide from white people, and pretending to befriend animals. It was a wonderful place for me as a child.

Adolescence was difficult. My sisters left for college and I felt abandoned. Suddenly my mother and I had no buffer between us. So I left, and wandered again, off to the woods. I would take a canteen of water, some crackers, and leave for the day. I was alone- I could pretend, imagine

153

and escape. I imagined being kidnapped by Indians, and learning about the woods, the animals, the plants. I was too engrossed in adolescent angst to notice much, but the trees gave me solace and healing. My father had played among these woods as a boy, and my grandfather remembered when a village of miners was there where now only trees and quiet existed. The history was healing, and the woods provided hope.

I left home at 18, but whenever I could, I escaped to the woods. Usually alone, I liked the solitude. I occasionally would see a deer, but never did I encounter anything scarier than a snake. Once I came across a shelter where two guys were living. They were students, studying forestry, and living in the woods. I was fascinated. How efficient! How interesting! How subversive! They did not have to pay rent. I wanted to live in the woods and never pay rent.

The day my father died a friend brought two sleeping bags and we spent the night out in the woods. Did I cry? Talk? Sleep? I do not know, but that was a gift of immeasurable value.

Through the decades of school, my profession, raising a family, getting a divorce, retiring – it has always been the woods that kept me whole and grounded. I experience the woods as a holy place of peace and prayer. The Divine Source has guided me and I could discern more clearly in the woods than other places. But I didn't know.

The birds, the trees, and the plants I could identify were the ones I learned as a child. White pine has five needles in a cluster, five letters to the word white. Maple, oak – but I didn't yet truly *know* them.

My first primitive skills school experience was six years ago. My adult children were involved and of course I wanted to share their experiences and learn what they loved about this place. So I drove north dreading it. I thought, 'really? Early May in the Maine woods? Blackflies. It could be hot or a frost and I cannot sleep on the ground. 'What am I doing?'

I arrived to the warmest, most respectful welcome I have ever received. I experienced a thanksgiving address, a string stalk, learning the seven points of awareness, and practiced foxwalking and owl eyes. I tried dead reckoning, building a debris hut, and starting a fire with a bow drill. Each experience was exhilarating, many were frustrating. The bowdrill did me in.

The climax was the drum stalk, an experience of awareness. Participants are instructed on how to safely walk in the woods alone at night – barefoot, off trail, blindfolded, and guided by the beating of a drum.

Words cannot define or interpret that holy experience. I was terrified but relaxed, afraid of making a fool of myself but confident that I was respected. I was fearful of getting lost but confident that amazing people knew where I was and would find me.

I returned from that weekend with a confidence I had never felt. I returned to work with a transcendent ability to function. I could ask hard questions, listen to people with new openness and challenge people to try new things. When my difficult supervisor would criticize and undermine my work, I would think to myself, "Yeah, let's see you do what I did". I am a woman who has walked in the woods, off trail, alone, at night, barefoot and blindfolded. I can do anything.

Sixty years ago my family asked, "Where's Linda?" Yesterday my adult kids and granddaughters asked, "Where's Linda?", and of course they knew to look for me in the woods. My experience in the woods has been enhanced, as I have learned the names and uses of trees and plants. The trees are my sisters and the plants are my allies. The more I learn, the more I realize how much there is to know, and I love that. There is so much to experience – the birds and their messages, the plants and their rhythms, the trees and their healing.

I am grateful for my father and grandfather, my mentors and teachers, and my family. I am grateful for this delicate and wonderful planet, and the waters of this planet that cleanse and renew. I am grateful for the plants that nourish and heal, and the creepy crawly things in the grasses, and the mosses and ferns. I am grateful for the trees and the winged ones who fly among them, and the four-legged ones who live in them. I am grateful for the sky with its sun and moon and stars and planets in their consistent courses. And I am grateful for Source of life and death, and life beyond death.

About Linda:

Linda Littlefield Grenfell is a wife, retired clergy, mother, and adjunct professor of philosophy. She lives in Maine where she happily resides with her husband, cat and dog and where she can walk out the door and be in the woods. Whether she is teaching or preaching she shares a passion for nature awareness, in hopes to increase commitment to address climate devastation. Through it all, she says "my dog loves me".

Free to Learn (One's Own) Nature

By

Tammy Gomez

The sky, the stars, the midnight moon, the leaves blowing towards the tiny cell window.

We are all aware of that poignant scene in movies or novels, where a sad prisoner looks mournfully, if wistfully, through the steel bars of the window, longing to stand unencumbered and free; free to walk under the wide open sky, to bend down and smell the wildest flowers, to listen appreciatively for cows lowing in the pastures, or to watch the occasional bumblebee buzzing towards nectar..

In that moment, we can understand the lonely desire of someone locked behind bars, tucked away in cinder block cells, kept from the nurturing joy of experiencing nature face to face. We might quietly sigh with contentment about our own relative freedom to stroll out the front door of our house to be consumed by a humid ambient breeze and be able to kneel on the earth, digging our fingers through fertile soil, and setting roots in garden plots, eyeing rainclouds in the distance.

We know what we are free to do, yet too many of us fail to explore that freedom. We seem to prefer locking ourselves indoors, with the electricity coursing through appliances and entertainment systems that keep us comfortable and sweat-free, almost anesthetized in insulated numbness.

Early in my life, however, I learned about sweat and work, about the pull on my ankles as I tugged myself uphill, following my father's steps as he led my sister, my mother, and me to where a cow lay with her newly-born calves. Daddy woke us at dawn. He pulled us out of our ranch house beds, to see this magical mystery in the meadow.

We didn't own the place, but merely resided in the big house in the middle of vast acreage where my father worked as the ranch foreman. We could look out my parents' bedroom windows and see lambs and goats roaming as they fed. We sometimes had to step lively from the car to the house so the geese wouldn't scare us as they gave chase. I rode in my dad's big blue pick-up truck and loved the sound of the engine as he threw it into second so we could manage the steep, rutted roads. I guess the rancher's life is ingrained in my blood, though once we moved to the city, I never saw animals beyond zoos and aquariums.

It was later, in my early 20's, that I reconnected with my nature self. I was living in Austin, and was surrounded in those mid-1980's days by hippies, who were mixing herb tinctures for medicine and introducing me to things like tofu, spirulina, and mineral water. As a Latina of Mexican descent, I moved like a chameleon among different cultural groups and pop trend associations, trying on affinities that my friends introduced and modeled. I knew that I wanted to be healthy and to move away from traditional habits - the lifestyle of mainstream assimilation - and I secretly loved that I was choosing to try things unpredictable.

Even after I graduated from a private liberal arts college in the northeast, I eschewed the path of careerism and financial success by moving back to Austin and co-housing with musicians, artists, and writers. For the first time, I realized that one could be college educated but consciously anti-materialistic. I soon took to the idea of pursuing quality of life experiences vs. quantity of material possessions. The Hill Country, where Austin is located, afforded plenty of ways to explore the outdoors on hikes and bicycle rides to swimming holes and camping spots where playful people rocked out all night to live local music. Reluctantly, we'd pile into our trucks and cars for the drive back to the city, already eager for the next time when we could get lost in nature again.

In the summer of 1986, my boyfriend and I took a long road trip up to Pennsylvania for a first-time experience at a Rainbow Gathering - the annual month-long camp-out of bacchanal meets nature lover festival. This sprawling event attracts hundreds of attendees, mostly young free-spirited free thinkers from all over the States, to a selected national forest each summer. That year, the Allegheny National Forest was our destination. Though we only stayed for a few days, I was struck by the kind curiosity demonstrated by everyone we passed and met along the dirt paths between encampments. I also noticed that hardly anyone wore watches; we were on Mother Nature's clock here. The Rainbow "family," as they are called, held several council meetings, and I noticed that the proceedings seemed reminiscent of Native American tribal gatherings, with folks passing a talking stick as they addressed the assembly. There seemed to be a great reverence for the idea of co-existing peacefully in concert with nature, and much attention and care was given to not trashing or polluting the forest with our presence. I was yet to learn terms like "sustainability," "eco-tourism," and "carbon footprint," but innately I felt the importance of treading lightly in this beautiful American forest with its huge trees and the tallest ferns I'd ever seen.

As my boyfriend and I wandered through the Gathering, we happened upon several young people erecting small rock sculptures in the shallow creek waters. I marveled upon seeing this sight because it seemed a creative way to engage with the land and her features. Too often people just race through parks and nature centers - largely focused on getting through a guided tour as efficiently as possible - without bothering to slow down and quiet their minds. In nature, any place can become a landmark, a go-to spot. All you have to do is stop, sit, crouch low to the earth, and allow the environment to delicately reveal the detail of itself.

The air quality that day in the forest was perfect, and I learned then and there that only away from the city fumes of industry and automobile congestion could my lungs and eyes be clear to do what I need them to do in my life. I breathed in as deeply as I could, vowing to store this commitment along with the air I took in: I will not contribute toxins to the environment, as much as I can help it.

The last great moment with the Rainbow family gave me a glimpse as to why they are called that: Near a lake at one edge of the forest, we saw people gathered for a huge OHM-ment, chanting together in one amazing vibrating tone of many voices as they held hands in a big circle. My boyfriend and I joined, as we needed no permission to participate. As the group's joyous chant swelled to a crescendo, the clouds I'd never noticed before split themselves open to spill a summer shower upon us. As the cooling rain splashed us and the earth, I trembled humbly with this new acknowledgment: Of course, the earth feels us moving and living upon it; of course, the universe desires a connection with human beings; of course, the natural resources we are given are fragile, magical gifts; and of course, it hears when we are grateful and celebratory in its majesty. And, then, as quickly as the shower began, it stopped so that we could notice one by one. We looked up to a rainbow - a spectrum of color and shine that buoyed our spirits and forever reminded me to never take rain, ferns, trees, soil, and all earthly sentient for granted.

Today, I still prefer to be outside, rather than indoors. I bicycle and do not drive. I grow edible plants in my front yard. I live a rich life of voluntary simplicity. And I will never be locked away from my own true nature, reflected and enhanced by my love and understanding of earth nature.

Imprisoned poets love nature.
A cell brings their spaciousness alive,
through air and no-space
dark and no-light
roof and no-tree
floor and no earth.

The imprisoned thinker
starts to savor rain
and butters his mind
with the fantasy flavors
of flowers, leaves,
and honeybees.
Drinking nectar is a rhyme
he writes in his mind,
she doesn't forget the nuance
of barefoot on grass
but she has to deliver
the feel through memory.

I too have been in box
closeted in no-light
with a realm of
dream and story to
make me the natural world
that can comfort.

I can cuddle with branches,
hunker down with lantana
when the cards are stacked high
against my uniformed neck.

They touch, these poets,
reaching for rock, listening
late-night to the howl of
a distant dog, singing with
the train, calling to the night, a
right way to beckon a simmering
and understanding breeze.

An imprisoned rebel pulls in a leaf
through the iron bars and selects
careful blood drips to ink his
song, and a drooping milkweed
seed can float onto her palm
so that it reminds her to read
the lifeline she manages to claim
in a place of stunted growth
and bedridden laughter.

This is the nature that the prisoner
brings in, allows through his locked
door and invites to his mouth.
Drops of his own tears remind of
the sea, as he/she/we

WOMEN IN NATURE

make plans
assert claims
dream new destinies
of desire

and she swears
and aspires to stop swimming in the metal
terror tremor of chains that keep her from knowing her true nature.

About Tammy

Currently based in Texas, Tammy Gomez is an award-winning poet (Best Poet of Austin, Austin Chronicle, 1997) and playwright/director. Her poems and essays have been anthologized widely, including in the Brooklyn Review, the Yellow Medicine Review, and Bicycle Love (Breakaway Books, 2004). For more information go to www.unitedstatesartists.org/user/tammygomez

WIN – Women in Nature

Books underway for 2014, 2015 and on...

WIN- Women in Nature on ADVENTURE

WIN- Women in Nature on ART

WIN- Women in Nature on CHILDREN

WIN- Women in Nature on COMMUNITY

WIN- Women in Nature on CREATURES OF THE SEA

WIN- Women in Nature on DWELLING

WIN- Women in Nature on EARTH'S ANIMALS

WIN- Women in Nature on ENERGY

WIN- Women in Nature on FOOD

WIN- Women in Nature on HEALING

WIN- Women in Nature on HUNTING (& fishing)

WIN- Women in Nature on INDIGENOUS CULTURE

WIN- Women in Nature on MUSIC & LANGUAGE

WIN- Women in Nature on PHILOSOPHY

WIN- Women in Nature on URBAN GARDENING

WIN- Women in Nature on WATER

...and more!

Thank you for sharing this journey with us.

We invite you to visit our website at <u>www.louisegracepublishing.com</u> and <u>www.WIN-womeninnature.com.</u>

And, ... to submit your stories!

Carol Clouse
Creative Director &
Production Designer

Carly Attanasio
Chief Editor &
Acquisitions Manager

Cathy Glass
Publicity &
Distribution Manager